THE SILENT QUEEN

WHY THE CHURCH NEEDS WOMEN TO FIND THEIR VOICE

PAUL ELLIS

KINGSPRESS

Beach Haven, New Zealand

The Silent Queen: Why the Church Needs Women to Find their Voice

ISBN: 978-1-927230-63-3
Copyright © 2020 by Paul Ellis

Published by KingsPress, P.O. Box 66145, Beach Haven 0749, New Zealand. This title comes with a study guide and is available in ebook and audiobook formats. For more information visit www.KingsPress.org.

All Scripture quotations, unless otherwise indicated, are taken from the Holy Bible, New International Version®, NIV®. Copyright © 1973, 1978, 1984, 2011 by Biblica, Inc.™ Used by permission of Zondervan. All rights reserved worldwide. www.zondervan.com The "NIV" and "New International Version" are trademarks registered in the United States Patent and Trademark Office by Biblica, Inc.™

Scripture quotations marked (AKJV) are taken from the American King James Version. Public domain.

Scripture quotations marked (MSG) are taken from The Message. Copyright © by Eugene H. Peterson 1993, 1994, 1995, 1996, 2000, 2001, 2002. Used by permission of NavPress. All rights reserved. Represented by Tyndale House Publishers, Inc.

Please note that KingsPress' publishing style capitalizes certain pronouns in Scripture that refer to the Father, Son, and Holy Spirit, and may differ from some publisher's styles. Some words in quoted scripture may also be italicized for emphasis.

Dedicated to my mother, Norma K. Ellis, who was living and breathing women in leadership long before I began writing about it.

Cover layout and design by Safeer Ahmed.

Version: 1.0 (December 2020)

Endorsements

If a book was ever needed, it's *The Silent Queen*. I was continually stunned by the things I discovered within the pages of this powerful book. It begs to be read by men and women alike, for when it is, it will expose lies, exalt truth and create real, lasting change.

- SANDRA McCOLLOM, author of *I Tried Until I Almost Died*

After reading *The Silent Queen*, you might find yourself convinced that God actually gave women voices because he intended for those voices to be heard. Why? Because Paul Ellis has taken every scripture that has been misapplied in order to silence women, as well as an abundance of passages that give accounts of women leaders and speakers, to thoughtfully, thoroughly, and theologically explain how God actually expects women to find their voices and use them. Thank you, Paul, for your partnership in the gospel and your dedication to spreading the really, really good news of God's grace.

- TRICIA GUNN, author of *Unveiling Jesus* and Founder of Parresia

In this book, Paul Ellis tears down the false idol that has been built in the church—the one where men are exalted above women and placed on a pedestal of pride that God never meant them to occupy. In his usual thorough, scripturally-centered, and grace-filled way, Paul cuts through the lies we've come to believe. He unpacks the true meaning of scriptures we've misread or that have been mistranslated, and he delivers truth in a way that sets us free to be who God calls us to be, whether we are male or female. I loved this book, and I learned heaps from it. I know you will too! Hey, you might even get set free as a result of reading it!

- LYN PACKER, author of *Daughters of Eve*

By limiting women, the church has unknowingly limited the impact of the gospel on the world. Thankfully, this is changing! Paul Ellis knocks it out of the park with his new book, *The Silent Queen*, giving both biblical support and a voice to women in ministry. It is an honor to endorse this critical and essential masterpiece for this generation.

-   NATE TANNER, evangelist at L3 International Ministries

Paul Ellis is a gifted writer, and *The Silent Queen* is a delight to read. Paul's case for women as leaders in the church and as equal partners in marriage is insightful, intelligent, and thoroughly thought out. *The Silent Queen* is an easy read, with a touch of humor, but the content is compelling.

-   MARGARET MOWCZKO, writer at MargMowczko.com

Brilliant! Amen! All this and more... above all, Yes! Really, the idea that any creation of God's should not be welcome to sing his praises is beyond me. Paul Ellis continues to speak truth and invites everyone back into the welcoming love of Jesus. You were never left out by God. All are welcome.

-   JAMI AMERINE, author of *Stolen Jesus* and *Well, Girl*

Contents

List of boxes

A Word Before

"My prayer is that all of them may be one, Father, just as we are one." – Jesus

I didn't write this book for women. Well, of course I wrote it for women. But not just women. I also wrote it for men who want to experience life to the full.

I wrote it for pastors who want healthy churches, and husbands who want radiant wives. I wrote it for parents who want happy families. I wrote it for my daughters and your daughters, and for my son and your sons.

I wrote this book so that we would stop swallowing the lies we've been sold, and so that we might enjoy the abundant life that has been offered to all of us.

In the words of Jesus, I wrote it that we might be one.

Grace and peace to you.

The Roar of the Lord

At dinner the other night, I asked my three daughters what they want to be when they grow up. My fifteen-year-old told me she wants to be an architect, my thirteen-year-old wants to design rockets for NASA, and my six-year-old wants to be a superhero. As a father, I'm thrilled that my girls are growing up in a world of unprecedented opportunity. They can become scientists, entrepreneurs, astronauts, surgeons, nurses, firefighters, diplomats, meteorologists, train drivers, and stay-at-home moms. They can do just about anything they want, as long as they don't aspire to preach, teach, or pastor a church.

Okay, that's not the whole picture.

My daughters can become superintendents in the Anglican Church, but not archbishops in the Catholic one. They can pastor a Methodist congregation, but not a Baptist one. As for teaching behind a pulpit or leading men, well, that depends.

Women and the church—now there's a complicated relationship. Research shows that women pray more, attend more, serve more, and are generally more spiritual than men. Yet if you have been in the church for any length of time, you've probably heard strange things said about women. Women must stay silent in church. Women were created to serve men. Divorced women are sinners. Women who remarry are sinners. Women who don't marry are odd. Childless women are not fulfilling God's plan for their lives. Women are more easily deceived by Satan. Women can teach children but not men. A woman must submit to her husband in all things, even if he is abusive. Women are equal as long as they do what they're told.

With messages like these, it's a wonder women even go to church!

The statements above are repugnant. If this is not obvious to you, try substituting the word women for any other group: Handicapped people are sinners. Immigrants must stay silent in church. Black people were created to serve.

See what I mean?

Hopefully you would never say such things, yet this is the sort of nonsense women hear all the time. It's called sexual discrimination, and when it comes wrapped in scripture it's an insidious evil. "The Bible says women can't speak, teach, or lead." Actually, the Bible says no such thing. "The husband is the head of the home, and the wife's role is to serve him and raise his children." The Bible doesn't say that either. Yet for 2,000 years, misguided men have cracked the whips of scripture to keep women in their place.

Enough is enough. For too long women have been rendered voiceless by a religious culture that treats them as second class.

It's time for men and women to speak up.

The $28,000,000,000 problem

In the bad old days, women were considered good for meal preparation and baby making but little more. Thankfully, those days are gone. Countries are increasingly governed by women presidents and prime ministers. Capable women run companies, universities, hospitals and departments. They conduct orchestras, write best-sellers, and create new technologies. They fly aircraft, drive spacecraft, and command armies. On movie screens, they clobber bad guys and save the world.

When you consider how far women have advanced, it's tempting to conclude that the war for equality is over. It isn't.

In a 2020 World Bank study of gender discrimination, only eight nations earned full marks for giving women the same legal rights as men.[1] *Eight!* That means 95 percent of countries don't treat women equally in the eyes of the law.

What century is this?

Sure, women have it better than they used to. But there's still a long way to go. Based on our current rate of progress, the World Economic Forum predicts the gender gap will not close for another 100 years.[2] This is a pity because according to a recent report by the McKinsey Global Institute, inequality costs us as much as $28 trillion, an amount comparable to the economies of the USA and China combined.[3]

Sexual discrimination hurts all of us, but it particularly hurts women. According to the World Health Organization, a third of all women have experienced some form of physical or sexual violence in their lives, usually at the hands of their partners.[4] One in five women will be married by the age of 18. This happens because in many countries girls are not valued as highly as boys, and marrying them off transfers their "economic burden" to another family.[5] And women are in greater danger of serious injury in a car crash, because safety features are designed for men.[6]

While I was writing this book, a man told me that I was late to the party, that the feminists have taken over the palace and women already dominate everything. Nothing could be further from the truth.

Take my home country, New Zealand, for example. We Kiwis pride ourselves on being champions of women's rights. We were the first nation to give women the right to vote, and we have elected several female heads of government. By law, women have the same education opportunities as men, and women outnumber men in our universities. New Zealand ranks sixth in the world for gender parity, well ahead of countries like Germany (10th), the United Kingdom (21st), and the United States (53rd). Many people consider New Zealand a benchmark for women's equality. We're a shining example for the rest of the world to follow.

As long as nobody mentions money.

In New Zealand, as in many countries, women earn less than men. This happens in part because women are more likely than men to assume child-raising responsibilities, and it also reflects the underrepresentation of women in senior positions and high-paying jobs. But even when you compare the income of women doing similar jobs to men, Kiwi women earn nearly 10 percent less than their male counterparts.[7] It may not sound like much, but over the course of a career in academia, that's a $300,000 penalty just for being a woman.[8]

And bear in mind that paying women less has been illegal in New Zealand for nearly fifty years. In other countries the wage gap is much bigger. In the United States, the typical woman earns only 80 percent of the typical male wage.[9] In addition to getting paid less for doing the same work, women are also more likely to get harassed and less likely to get promoted.

That's in the workplace. How are things at home?

In New Zealand, a quarter of women can expect to be sexually assaulted in their lifetimes, and one out of five girls will experience unwanted sexual contact. Women are also three times as likely as men to be the victims of intimate partner violence, and this in a country that treats women better than most.[10]

The war for equality and fairness is far from over. But what about in the church?

Women in the church

Since its inception, the church has championed the rights of women. It has done this by opposing polygamy, incest, and underage marriage; promoting women's education; caring for widows and orphans; and proclaiming the dignity of every person. While the pagan world was visiting upon women every form of injustice and depravity known to man, the church was providing a refuge and a hope for a better future. This is a track record we can be proud of.

But do women in the church enjoy the same opportunities as men?

Women make up more than half of the church but account for less than ten percent of its senior leaders. By leader, I mean pastors or priests leading congregations. In the church we allow women to minister a hundred different ways—they serve in the crèche, sing in the choir, and cook the potluck dinners—but we don't allow them to lead. Which is surprising, because studies reveal that many of us have no problem accepting female priests or pastors in theory. But in practice, it's a different story. Even churches that aren't opposed to women in leadership are reluctant to hire them because doing so can lead to division and strife.

There is no question the church has made positive strides in recognizing women in leadership. Up until the 1950s, there were very few women in recognized ministry. But any positive trend has been mostly at the grassroots level. In the Catholic Church, for instance, women lay ministers are common, but women priests are not. In the American Protestant Church, only nine percent of senior protestant pastors are women.[11]

From time to time, some report will come out in the Christian media trumpeting the rapid growth in the percentage of female pastors or preachers. "Number of clergywomen has exponentially increased over last two decades," claimed a recent headline in *The Christian Post*.[12] But when your starting point is zero, any increase looks good. The fact is we are not remotely close to achieving parity. Maybe in another hundred years. Maybe my granddaughters' granddaughters will see it.

Surveys reveal that women feel called to lead in equal numbers as men, yet senior male leaders outnumber women eleven to one. God distributes his gifts liberally to all, but the priesthood remains a male-dominated club. Denying women the opportunity to exercise their gifts may explain why a third of them say they are resigned to low expectations.[13] They are not fulfilled in the church, and they know they never will be.

Perhaps God has given you the ability to preach and teach. Maybe you have a story to tell or a desire to lead. If you are a woman who desires to be faithful to the call of God, you can expect opposition in the form of religious tradition. You will be told you can share but not preach. You can speak in the small group but not the large one. You can serve coffee but not communion. You need a husband or some sort of male covering. You better not wear trousers and for heaven's sake don't show emotion. Break these rules and you will be marginalized, silenced, and branded a Jezebel.

It is sometimes remarked that the modern church is excessively feminine, which is ironic given the way we treat women. We fret about the shortage of men in the pews but give no thought to the absence of women in the pulpit. We bend over backwards to attract new men but do little to promote the women who are already here.

The roar of the Lord

I like to think that I am an easy-going guy, but a funny thing happened during the writing of this book. The more I wrote, the angrier I got. I blame the women. Knowing that I was writing a book about them, female readers began sharing with me their stories of how they have been treated in the church. "I was told that I could not read the Bible aloud to my husband because it's the man's job to teach." "My husband was abusive, but the church leaders said I should stay with him and forgive him." "I started a prayer group, and once it started growing, one of the elders thought it would be more fitting for him to take over since he was male."

Others told me some of the horrendous lines they had heard from the pulpit. "If a man looks at you with lust, it's your fault." "You must ask your husband's permission before cutting your hair." "You can't lead—you're a woman. Get back to the kitchen." "A woman needs to prepare and have a schedule for pleasing her husband, just as she does for making his meals." A woman who asked questions was rebuked for challenging the leadership team and told to "go back to making sandwiches."

Hearing these stories, I didn't know whether to laugh or cry at the absurdity of it all. I had no idea. I suspect most men don't. We are oblivious to the systemic sexism that women deal with all the time.

Several women told me they were done with church. "I don't want my daughters hearing this stuff," said one, except she didn't use the word stuff. I found it hard to disagree with her. I wouldn't want my daughters hearing this stuff either.

God forgive us for the things we have done to his daughters. We have killed their dreams, extinguished their gifts, and diminished their humanity. Instead of preaching a different message from the world, we have perpetuated an ancient and evil bias. Instead of hearing what God says to us through women, we have told them to be quiet and return to the kitchen.

In his book *Ten Lies the Church Tells Women*, Lee Grady offers a scathing assessment of the gender prejudice in our churches:

> For centuries the church has taught godly women that they must quench the holy fire of God that burns within them. As a result, half the labor force in the church has been sidelined and devalued. And while women have been disqualified from the game and sent to the bench, we men have arrogantly told our sisters in Christ that this is God's perfect plan.[14]

If there's such a thing as righteous anger, I can feel it in my bones. Behind the chorus of injustice, I can hear the roar of the Lord. According to the prophets of old, the roar of the Lord is meant to gather and galvanize his people. "They will follow the Lord; he will roar like a lion. When he roars, his children will come."[15]

I don't think I have ever heard a sermon on the roar of the Lord. Have you? We are more likely to hear how the devil is like a roaring lion looking for someone to devour.[16] Since the beginning of human history, the enemy has sought to thwart God's plans for partnership by promoting strife between men and women. That old liar seeks to devour and destroy, but when the true Lion of Judah roars that old imposter turns tail and flees.

The Lord roars against the enemies attacking his daughters. He raises his voice against sexual exploitation, domestic violence, trafficking, rape, molestation, honor killings, spousal abuse, and femicide. He thunders against injustice and the lies preached in his name.

If the righteous are as bold as a lion, as the proverb says, it is time for the righteous to roar the roar of the Lord. This is not the time to close our eyes and pretend all is well. This is the time to speak for those who have been silenced.

Catherine Booth, cofounder of the Salvation Army, once said, "If we are to better the future we must disturb the present." To right a wrong, we must make a ruckus, and a ruckus I plan to make. Will you join me? Do you hear the roar of the Lord?

Three views about women

Each of us holds a view about the role of women. What can they do; what can't they do? Your answers to these questions defines your bias. We may think that our biases are informed by scripture, but often it is the other way around. We come to the Bible wearing certain lenses, and what we look through determines what we see.

Before we dive deeper, it will help if we identify three lenses or perspectives the church has towards women. First, there is the traditional or hierarchical view that says women are inferior to men. This was the line taken by theologians who said women were created in the image of men rather than God. Since she is inferior by design, a woman's role is to serve her husband, and she can never lead. "A woman, however learned and holy, may not take upon herself to teach in an assembly of men," said the men of the Fourth Synod of Carthage.[17]

Then there is the complementarian view that says women are equal in value but unequal in role. In the same way a child is equal but subordinate to a parent, a wife is subordinate to her husband or church leaders. The complementarian view differs from the traditional perspective in that it affirms the equality of women, but it reinforces old stereotypes about men being natural-born leaders. "Some governing and teaching roles within the church are restricted to men," says one complementarian website.[18] In the home as in the church, men lead and women follow.

Finally, there is the egalitarian view that says God made men and women equal in every way—they are equal in value and equal in role. Since men and women were given joint responsibility to rule over creation, both can lead. This is not to deny the differences between the genders or to suggest those differences are unimportant. But to quote the Christians for Biblical Equality website, the egalitarian view recognizes that "God calls women and men of all cultures, races, and classes to share authority equally in service and leadership in the home, church, and world."[19]

Which are you? Are you a traditionalist, a complementarian, or an egalitarian? What we label, we diminish, but if I had to choose between these perspectives, I would be unashamedly egalitarian. I'm a Kiwi married to a Dane; how could I not be? But I am not a rabid egalitarian. On the one hand, I am convinced that equality protects us from the abuses of hierarchy and the misuse of authority. But on the other, I fear the dogged pursuit of equality can hinder authentic relationships.

Like a referee, equality is essential, but it's not the game. It is not the ultimate goal. For the Christian, the higher goal is love.

Jesus never said his disciples would be known for their equality and sense of fair play. We are to be known for the way we serve, respect, and prefer one another. If we settle for equality, there's a danger we will fall short of all that God has in store for us, particularly in our marriages.

Equality is not the end game in the war on gender discrimination; it's the starting point for the new creation. Equality is a good thing, but what we do with it is far more important. I look forward to the day when my daughters have the same opportunities as my son, but I'm much more interested in what they will do with those opportunities. Imagine a church where women get the same respect and take on the same roles as men. Actually, you don't need to imagine such a church at all. Just read the Book of Acts, and you will see that a church where all are valued can change the world. It happened before, and it can happen again.

The roadmap

Like a car towing a caravan, this book has two parts. In Part A, we will climb into the metaphorical DeLorean for a trip down the highways of history. Our journey begins in the Garden of Eden where we will discover God's original roadmap for men and women. Like rubberneckers on the freeway, we will watch in horror as his beautiful plan gets T-boned by sin. We will sift through the wreckage with the patriarchs of Israel and the philosophers of Greece, and we'll sit on the roadside with the sore and silent queens of the Bible. We'll discuss remedies with the rabbis and therapies with the theologians, but all we will learn is how some of the world's smartest men have perpetuated the dumbest ideas we've inherited about women.

But our tour is not all doom and gloom. A highlight of our journey will be a first-century detour to see Jesus redeem God's glorious plan. We will hear the roar of the rushing wind as the Holy Spirit empowers the early church to walk in unity, and we will witness the glorious things that happen when men and women partner together in the pattern prescribed by God. By the time we reach the end of our journey, we will have mapped out a course to take us into a better and brighter future.

In the second part of this book, we will park the caravan and gather round the campfire to discuss some of the thorniest issues afflicting womankind. Some of these debates are centuries old. What can we possibly say that hasn't been said a hundred times before? The issues are ancient, but our discussion will be seasoned with new covenant grace. We will read old scriptures through the lens of the new creation, and we will toss upon the flames those traditions that keep women silent.

I hope you are excited to begin our journey. Before we depart, here's a question for the road. The scriptures say we are God's chosen people and a royal priesthood.[20] You are not a servile priest but a royal one, called to rule and reign. So here's my question: What makes a man a king or a woman a queen? A man is not a king because he is lords it over others and vanquishes all foes with his manly performance. Nor is he a king because his woman kowtows before him and his children revere him. He is a king because Jesus makes him so.[21]

The same is true for women. A woman is not a queen because her husband treats her well or because men fear sexual harassment lawsuits. A woman is a queen because her Kingly Father has made her so. As a child of the most high, you are royalty.

A woman who knows the call of God will reign in life. She will not be silenced or sidelined by scriptures taken out of context, nor will she be perturbed by prejudice and patriarchy. Such a woman does not need men to get with the program, and she has no intention of waiting a hundred years for the scales to balance. Since her confidence comes from her heavenly Father, she cannot be shaken, and she prospers in everything she does.

To the women reading this, you have a voice. God has given you a song, a story, a message. He has written it in your members and weaved it into your story. The world needs to hear what you have to say. My prayer is that in these pages you will encounter the love of God, and his grace will give you the confidence to speak boldly. May his song be in your heart and his praises be upon your lips. May your testimony bring hope and freedom to many.

To the men reading this, we need to hear what God is saying to us through the women in our lives. We will be blessed if we do. Let us repent for past hurts, and let us speak for those who cannot speak for themselves. My prayer is that we will rise up as champions for our wives, daughters, sisters, and mothers. May we encourage them to speak, and may we have the grace to hear what they say.

Part A: The Story of Men and Women

1. Your Royal Invitation

In the beginning, God made everything and the last thing he made, the culmination of his creation, was a woman. Why did God make women? Contrary to what you may have heard, women were not made to be servants for God or men. God had something far more glorious in mind:

> So God created mankind in his own image, in the image of God he created them; male and female he created them. God blessed them and said to them, "Be fruitful and increase in number; fill the earth and subdue it. Rule over the fish in the sea and the birds in the sky and over every living creature that moves on the ground." (Genesis 1:27–28)

This passage is a treasure box of gems, such as this: women and men were *made by God*. You are not an accident or an inferior product. You're a one-of-a-kind masterpiece. Don't ever think you are the wrong sort of person or the wrong shape, color, or gender. You are fearfully and wonderfully made by a Creator who only makes good things.

Not only were you made by God; you were made in his image. There is a touch of the divine about you, something indisputably Godlike. Unlike the animals, you are a spiritual, intellectual, and relational being with a creative streak inherited from your heavenly Father. This is why we humans are capable of making the most extraordinary things: symphonies, sonnets, stories, skyscrapers, submarines and spaceships. Most wondrously, we have the ability to create life, from new people to new societies and civilizations.

On account of your Father, you are royal. You have been given heavenly authority to king-down upon your circumstances. Whether you are a man or a woman, the problems of this world are yours to tread upon.

Why did God make you? You were made to be the object of the Father's love and affection. You may not know this but it's true. God is love, and love requires expression. It's not that God was incomplete without you. But out of the exceeding abundance of his love, he wanted a *you* in his universe, and here you are. God is smiling at you and he delights in you. He is absolutely thrilled that you are here.

Another gem: you have been called by God to be fruitful and rule over the earth. It's a lofty thought, but what does that mean? In the beginning of the Bible, the details are vague. It's only later through his prophets, poets, and psalmists that God begins to reveal pictures of the kingdom to come. But in Genesis we get a hint. Fill the earth. Reproduce and recreate. Raise families and train disciples. Impart and equip. Two children were never going to be enough for a Father with a God-sized capacity for love. He wants a big family, and the bigger the better.

How do we bear fruit and fill the earth? In partnership. Notice how God blessed *them* and spoke to *them*. Some of life's richest blessings are experienced in our togetherness. This is not obvious to those of us who have been raised with a me-first mentality. We've been told to stand on our own two feet, believe in ourselves, fight our own fights, and chart our own course. But the cost of independence is often loneliness and barrenness. Chart your own course and you could end up lost.

"It is not good for man to be alone," God said. We need each other, especially if we are to be fruitful and multiply.[1] God blesses us in our partnerships, and the result is we bear fruit and fill the earth.

The divine call to partnership

Partnership is a theme of this book because it's a theme of God's book. It's the thread running through the entire tapestry. Have you ever noticed how some of the greatest characters in the Bible had partners? Moses and Aaron, Deborah and Barak, Naomi and Ruth, Peter and John, Priscilla and Aquila. David had his mighty men. Paul had Barnabas, Luke, Timothy, Silas and others. Jesus had the twelve apostles. The Bible is a we-book rather than a me-book. Go through Paul's letters highlighting the corporate words *we, you,* and *your,* and you will hardly find a verse that does not reference our togetherness.

The biblical kings knew about the blessings of partnership. "How good and pleasant it is when God's people live together in unity!" said King David. "Two are better than one," said King Solomon. "Where two or three gather in my name, there am I," said King Jesus.[2]

Even in the creation story we see partnership. God said, "Let us make man in our image."[3] Who is *us*? Nobody knows for sure.[4] But it seems that God, working in partnership, made a pair of partners, and those partners made more partners and so on and so forth. At the end of this long unbroken line of partnerships is you. You are living proof that life comes through partnership.

As in the natural, so in the spiritual. God designed you to be connected to him so that together you might release his life-giving blessing to others. If that sounds weird, here is a word that may help: *koinonia.* This word is found throughout the New Testament, and it is usually translated as fellowship. It literally means partnership.[5] *Koinonia* describes the union believers have with each other and the Lord. *Koinonia*-partnership is about living joyfully out of our connection with Christ and his body. It's the recipe for the abundant life that flows from the fullness of his love. It's the freedom to know and be known, to give and receive, to love and be loved. *Koinonia* is about being blessed in our togetherness. And it comes straight out of Genesis 1.

God blessed *them.*

Your golden ticket

God's words about ruling and filling the earth ought to be printed in gold letters, for they are a royal invitation, a golden ticket to the life you were made for. To paraphrase the Apostle Paul, you are destined to reign.[6] But it only happens in partnership.

What does partnership look like? In the opening chapters of the Bible, we see a man and a woman joined to each other in a special arrangement we call marriage. "Two shall become one."[7] Two people, one partnership. As the narrative unfolds, we get more pictures of partnership: families, friends, tribes, nations, disciples, ministry teams, communities, churches.

The central message of this book is that you and I and every one of us have been invited to participate in a divine partnership. Biblical partnership can be defined as living in union with Christ as a healthy and active member of his body. As we abide in him, we bear fruit that lasts. Apart from him, we can do nothing.

Why all this talk about partnership in a book about women? Because God's plan for the first man and woman is his plan for you and me. His plan hasn't changed. We were born to rule and reign, to be the head and not the tail, and to walk this world with the affirmation of the Creator who loves us. His plan is for all of us, regardless of race or gender.

Now pause for a moment, and compare this call to partnership with the message you may have heard: Women are second-class. Women are here to serve. Women are meant to be seen and not heard. Women can go so far but no further.

Traditionally, the world has placed limits on what women can and can't do, but look at the Creator's words in Genesis 1, and you find no limits. The sky is the limit. If the Almighty invites women to rule the earth, there is nothing they can't do.

In this book, we will examine several scriptures that seem to contradict the Creator's claim. Seem to, but don't. We will find that contrary to what tradition has taught us, these scriptures emphatically reinforce God's invitation for us to walk in partnership with him and each other.

C.S. Lewis once said that grace separates Christianity from every other religion. The grace of God is certainly special, but it is not the only thing that makes Christianity unique. How about partnership? No other religion portrays marriage as a holy partnership between two equals and their God. And no other religion has done more to promote the equality of men and women. Living out of *koinonia*-partnership is the very essence of the Christian life.

Yet we can hardly congratulate ourselves for our treatment of women. For 2,000 years, the church has treated half its members poorly, and the world is unfathomably poorer for it. The strange thing is we know better. We know that when one part of the body tells another part, "You are inferior," the whole body suffers.[8] Yet we seem incapable of breaking the destructive pattern.

God never intended for men to rule over women or for his daughters to be treated as anything less than queens. We were created as equals, male and female, to rule together in a royal partnership.

So what went wrong?

2. The Silent Queen

Recently in New Zealand, there was a job advertisement calling for a couple to manage a holiday camp. According to the ad, the ideal wife would have knowledge of Microsoft Office, know how to work the telephone, and be "of a quiet disposition." The implication was that vocal or outspoken wives would not be suitable for the job.[1]

The ad created no small stir because in New Zealand we consider ourselves egalitarian when it comes to women's rights. In fact, it is against the law to discriminate on the basis of gender. (The man who placed the ad backpedaled in the face of public reaction.) The ad was more amusing than harmful, but it raises an interesting question. How did we arrive at the notion that a good wife is a quiet wife?

"A silent wife is a gift from the Lord," said Ben Sira, a Jewish scribe who lived 200 years before Christ. A man fortunate to be married to a good and silent wife "will live twice as long because of her."[2]

Sage advice. But from where did Ben Sira get this idea that the ideal wife is silent? Perhaps he got it from the story of Adam and Eve.

Eve was the first woman to speak in the Bible. She uttered a few sentences, then she never spoke again. Or at least, no more of her words were deemed worthy of being recorded.

"Better that she should not have spoken at all," Ben Sira might have said. "For the little she did say led us into a world of hurt." He's not wrong. Adam got into trouble, said God, because he listened to the voice of his wife.[3]

Who was this Eve who spoke to the serpent? Tradition tells us she was a temptress who seduced her husband into sin. At best, she was foolish; at worst, she was in cahoots with the devil. Look at any painting of Adam and Eve, and chances are she's beguiling her husband with the forbidden fruit.

Bad, wicked Eve. She should've kept her mouth shut. Like a good wife from the Lord. Like a campground manager's wife.

Would the real Eve please stand up?

We need to take another look at the first woman. The Bible says little about Eve, but the little it says is too important to miss.

Along with her husband, Eve was called by God to rule over the earth. Which means Eve was a queen. Indeed, she was *the Queen* and the mother of all the kings and queens who came after her.

Yet if you Google "queens of the Bible," you will not find Eve's name on any list of royalty.

Why not?

Maybe it's because her name is stained with scandal. Eve was the queen who fell. She heeded the serpent and lost her right to reign.

Tradition tells us that Eve was alone when she was seduced by the devil. If her manly husband had been around, the crafty serpent would never had tried his dirty tricks. Yet the lonely wife interpretation doesn't square with the biblical account. When the serpent spoke to Eve, her husband was right there with her.[4] So Eve can hardly shoulder all the blame for what happened next. The serpent prevailed because the husband-wife partnership failed to recognize the danger they were in. At least Queen Eve tried to refute the liar. But acting alone, she was no match for the serpent's cunning.

After the Fall, Eve seems to have been struck from the historical record. Almost nothing she says or does is recorded. Adam had sons who became city-builders and men of renown, but Eve and her daughters were shunted to the side. The men of ancient times were kings and conquerors, but the women did nothing worth writing about. After Eve, the words of no woman are recorded in scripture for more than a thousand years.

To the woman he said, "I will make your pains in childbearing very severe; with painful labor you will give birth to children. Your desire will be for your husband, and he will rule over you." (Genesis 3:16)

These are God's words, but this was never God's plan. God wanted Adam to rule with Eve, not over her. He wanted their partnership to bear fruit with joy, not pain.

In Genesis 1 we were ordained to be kings and queens, but in Genesis 3 we lost our crowns. The divinely-mandated partnership between men and women was dissolved by selfishness and sin. God offered us abundant life, but we chose death.

As a result of the Fall, Eve lost her identity and her voice.[5] She went from being co-ruler to being ruled, from a queen to a subject. "Your desire will be for your husband." From now on, Eve would find value in the aid she gave to the men in her life. Her sense of self-worth would come from being a good wife and a hardworking mother. "He will rule over you," meaning Adam and his sons would have the last word and the final say. They would make the decisions and write the rules. They would create history while their wives raised their children.

Adam and Eve's rebellion created an unequal division of labor that persists to this day. Even in the church. Rank your top ten preachers and teachers and chances are most of them are men. Rank history's most influential pastors, evangelists, missionaries, and authors, and you'll get the same result. The majority are men. Where are the women? They're either playing the supportive wife, or they're sitting silently on the sidelines. For sure, there are notable exceptions, but women who speak with authority are notable precisely because they are exceptions. Like the women who speak in the Bible, they're in the minority (see Box 2.1: The unnamed women of the Bible).

God told Eve she was destined to reign, and one way we rule is by speaking. When the Creator spoke, his creative will shaped a formless and chaotic world. But Eve misspoke and became the silent queen. Ever since the Fall, her daughters have been silenced by the men who rule them. "Don't teach, don't preach, but if you really must talk, be accountable to a man."

The Fall of humanity was the worst thing that ever happened to us. God created a partnership of equals, but sin sent our world spiraling into a self-destructive tailspin of misogyny and discrimination. The consequences were catastrophic, but for the sake of brevity we will examine just two of the evils that replaced partnership, namely polygyny and patriarchy.

Box 2.1: The unnamed women of the Bible

The Bible is populated with a large cast of colorful characters, from kings to knaves. What is the proportion of male to female roles in scripture? If God's plan for partnership had come to pass, we might expect an equal split between men and women. In fact, women account for only a small minority of the people named in the Bible, less than eight percent.[6]

Think of Noah's Ark. The Bible records the names of the four men on the ark, but not their wives. These women endured the same trial as the men, but they are nowhere named. They are simply wives. Identifying significant women by their relationship to their men is a common pattern in scripture. Thus we have the unnamed wives of Job, Phinehas, Potiphar, and Pilate; the unnamed daughters of Lot, Zelophehad, and Jepthah; and the unnamed mothers of Jabez and Samson.

Women's names are omitted from the biblical record and so are their words. In the Bible, 71 women have speaking parts. It sounds like a large group, yet the words of women account for barely one percent of all the words spoken in scripture. And half of the women with speaking parts do not have their names recorded. They're anonymous. Two of the most vocal women in the Bible, accounting for nearly 20 percent of all the words spoken by women, are the unnamed Shulammite woman and the Woman of Tekoa.[7]

Polygyny replaces partnership

God intended for marriage to be between one man and one woman, but Adam's offspring took multiple wives, a practice known as polygyny. (Polygyny is a kind of polygamy. The other kind—having multiple husbands—is known as polyandry.)

Polygyny was common among the ancients. A few generations after Adam, Lamech became the first recorded polygynist in history when he took two wives. Jacob and Esau had two wives at the same time, as did Samuel's father Elkanah. King David was a polygynist, while his son Solomon was the most infamous polygynist of all. Herod the Great, who tried to murder baby Jesus, had nine wives.[8]

Interestingly, the Law of Moses legitimized polygyny but not polyandry. A man could have several wives, but a woman could not have several husbands.[9] Josephus, the Jewish historian, noted it was a custom of the Jews to have many wives.[10]

What does polygyny have to do with us? The old custom of polygyny casts a shadow on the modern church whenever we discuss divorce. By failing to grasp the historical context of polygyny, we tend to misread the words of Jesus and Paul. As a result, divorced people, and especially divorced women, are wrongly condemned as sinners. More on this later. For now, it is sufficient to note that polygyny is at odds with God's plan because it exalts a husband above his wives. He is no longer an equal partner in a matched pair but a little king ruling his harem. He has become a patriarch.

And so does patriarchy

We honor the patriarchs of the Bible, and rightly so. But we must also acknowledge that any system where men hold all the power is contrary to God's plan of partnership.

Patriarchy literally means the rule of the father, and it is the oldest and most enduring form of gender discrimination. Patriarchy sounds benevolent, especially to those who have been raised by loving fathers. But its inherent imbalance can lead to the mistreatment of women. Just ask Lot's daughters what they thought of their father offering them to the lecherous men of Sodom. Ask Hagar how she felt about being used as a surrogate mother before being fired by her employer Abraham. Ask the Levite's concubine what it was like to be offered to a mob of rapists.[11]

Nearly every culture practices some form of patriarchy, but scholars disagree over its origins. Some say patriarchy is a consequence of biology (women are stuck at home raising the kids while the men conquer the world). Others look to anthropological and historical causes. But patriarchy comes straight out of Genesis 3. It's the fruit of sin.

Patriarchy is oppressive to women, yet many Christian women accept it because they've been told it's biblical. "The husband is the head of the home and his wife is his helper." Such claims are derived from scripture, but they are no more biblical than slavery and genocide. In the second part of this book, we will look at what the Bible says about helpers and headship, but rest assured that nothing in the New Testament contradicts what God says in Genesis 1.

Patriarchy is demeaning to women, but patriarchy also hurts men. By weakening our queens it weakens our marriages and families. By silencing our wives, it makes it harder for us to hear God's voice.

Patriarchy clips the wings of our partnerships and deprives us of countless blessings.

Is the Bible sexist?

Some people reject the Bible because they believe it promotes a male-dominated worldview. "The Bible is oppressive to women. It reinforces patriarchal stereotypes that view women as inferior." There is a measure of truth to this claim.

Take the laws of Israel. Israel had laws that permitted the kidnapping of foreign women, and prescribed conditions under which a rape victim could be compelled to marry her rapist. Under the law, a man could overrule his wife or daughter's vow, and an impoverished father could sell his daughter as a concubine. By law, only men could work as priests and serve in the temple.[12]

But to reject the Bible because it provides an accurate portrayal of patriarchal cultures is to throw out the baby with the bathwater. The Bible also champions the role of women. It honors female pioneers and leaders. The Bible empowers and elevates women in many different ways.

The Fall of man created patriarchy, but this skewed arrangement was never God's plan. Consider the gender equality promoted in the Ten Commandments. The fifth commandment is honor your father *and mother*. Your parents are worthy of equal honor.

Or consider the fourth commandment, which institutes a day of rest for your son *and daughter*, your male *and female* servant.[13] Again, equality. In an age where women were considered property, God defended their rights. "Treat your mothers like your fathers and your daughters like your sons."

The Ten Commandments are among the oldest laws protecting women's rights. They formalize God's heart for an equal partnership between men and women.

So why the inconsistency in Israel's laws? Why is there one set of laws (the Ten Commandments) promoting equality and another (the 600+ miscellaneous laws) promoting discrimination? Perhaps it is because the world is a messy place. What God gives, men take away.

Is the Bible sexist? No, but we are, and the Bible portrays this. The Bible also reveals the good heart of our Maker. Men write the rules and rig the game, but in God's eyes women are equal partners. This was true even in the old covenant.

A man by the name of Zelophehad died leaving five daughters. Their names were Mahlah, Noah, Hoglah, Milcah and Tirzah. In those days, it was the custom for sons to inherit land while daughters got dowries. Not these ladies. "We want our inheritance," they said to Moses. To his credit, Moses brought their case before the Lord, and the Lord told Moses to give them their land.

Stories like this remind us that God's view of women is often different from ours. Cultures come and go, but God never changes. He created both male and female in his image, and his desire has always been for us to rule and reign together in partnership.

The ancient Israelites were patriarchal, but so was everybody else. Virtually every culture believed that women were inferior to men and subject to their rule. Yet one group had a profound influence on the modern world. The men in this tribe polished the idol of patriarchy and made it respectable. They taught the world how to oppress women and they laid the foundation for a corrupt Christian worldview. Who were these sexist teachers?

They were the Athenians.

3. Athenian Supermen

How would you rate the most influential people in history? This is the question behind an ongoing study being run by MIT's Media Lab. In this study, influence is measured by counting the number of page views on Wikipedia biographies. The more times a biography is read, the more influential the person.

A while back the folks at MIT reported that the most influential person in history was the Greek philosopher Aristotle. In second place was Plato, third was Jesus, and fourth was Socrates. Alexander the Great ranked fifth.[1] Why is this significant? Because four of the five most influential people in history believed that women are inferior to men.

Why women?

The Bible teaches that women were made as an expression of God's love. The Greeks had a different perspective. Apparently, Zeus created women to punish uppity men. Men were becoming too clever and needed to be taken down a peg. So the gods created women to harass and trouble them.[2]

Women are cunning and deadly, said the Greeks. They are the ultimate cause of suffering and heartache. They are the source of all evil. **Semonides** of Amorgos said women are "the worst plague Zeus ever made."[3] The poet **Hesiod** said, "Whoever puts his trust in a woman puts his trust in tricksters." He then added that each man should get himself a woman, but not as a wife. "I mean a woman that you own as a slave."[4]

Since women are deceptive and dangerous, they need to be ruled by a firm male hand. This was the position taken by **Homer**, he of the *Odyssey* fame. A wise man, said Homer, "gives law to his children and wives."[5]

Homer lived around 800 years before Christ, and his words would have been lost to us except the Athenians recorded them for posterity. The Athenians also provided us with the most influential philosophers of western civilization. Socrates (470–399BC), Xenophon (431–354BC), Plato (427–347BC) and Aristotle (384–322BC) laid the foundations for much of what we believe about women.

Which is a crying shame.

Socrates was relatively progressive in his beliefs that women should be educated, but he also said that women were inferior to men in terms of "their judgment and physical strength."[6] In his *Republic* he opined that "all the pursuits of men are the pursuits of women also, but in all of them a woman is inferior to a man."[7]

Xenophon, a student of Socrates, was one of the first to say a woman's place is in the home. "Since (God) has made (a woman's) body less capable of such endurance, I take it that God has assigned (her) the indoor tasks."[8] Many churchmen would agree with him.

Plato, another student of Socrates, said that men were the superior sex and warned that lazy, flawed men would be reincarnated as women:

He that has lived his appointed time well shall return again to his abode in his native star, and shall gain a life that is blessed and congenial, but whoso has failed therein shall be changed into woman's nature at the second birth.[9]

Plato's student **Aristotle** also taught that women were inferior to men: "The male is by nature superior and the female inferior; the male ruler and the female subject."[10]

It takes a special kind of intellect to say that women are substandard humans and defective by design, yet Athens was blessed to have two such minds. Plato and Aristotle may have been intellectual giants, but when it came to women, they were Tweedledum and Tweedledummer. Of the two, Aristotle was worse. While Plato believed women could be made useful through education, Aristotle held no such hope. He said women were like animals who needed men to tame them:

> Tame animals have a better nature than wild, and all tame animals are better off when they are ruled by man; for then they are preserved. Again, the male is by nature superior, and the female inferior; and the one rules, and the other is ruled; this principle, of necessity, extends to all mankind.[11]

Women are inferior, weaker, less capable, and just plain dumber than men. So said the most influential thinkers in western civilization.

With men like these running the show, ancient Greece was no place to be a woman. The young girls of Athens essentially had three career paths: they could become mothers, household servants, or high-class hookers called *hetairai*. If they chose the first and least objectionable option, they would be married off in their early teens and spend the rest of their uneducated lives cloistered away in their husband's homes. They would not participate in civic life and their names would rarely be mentioned in public.

To live in Athens was a demeaning existence for women, but **Alexander the Great** (356–323BC) thought the city was the pinnacle of civilization. Having been tutored by Aristotle, Alexander exported the Athenian model around the world in a process known as Hellenization. If you've ever wondered why the New Testament was written in Greek, you can thank the energetic Alexander. Israel, along with much of the Roman Empire, had been Hellenized. Educated Jews spoke Greek as a second language. And like the Greeks, the Jews treated their women little better than slaves.

Patriarchy becomes religion

In a world of darkness and depravity, the nation of Israel was meant to be a beacon for justice and equality. But by the time Jesus arrived, the Jewish view of women was not much different from the

Athenian one. Like the Greek philosophers, the rabbis and scribes taught that women were untrustworthy, inferior to men, and not worth educating (see Box 3.1: The Jewish view of women at the time of Jesus).

Box 3.1: The Jewish view of women at the time of Jesus

"The birth of a daughter is a loss."

"Whoever teaches his daughter Torah teaches her lasciviousness."

"Man's wickedness is better than a woman's goodness."

"A woman's voice is nakedness, and one may not speak with her."

"A man may sell his daughter, but a woman may not sell her daughter."

"Women's wisdom is solely in the spindle."

"Blessed are you, O God and King, who has not made me a Gentile, a slave, or a woman."

Sources[12]

The Ten Commandments promoted gender equality, but in the hands of fallen men these good laws were twisted into tools of feminine oppression. Consider the tenth commandment:

You shall not covet your neighbor's wife. You shall not set your desire on your neighbor's house or land, his male or female servant, his ox or donkey, or anything that belongs to your neighbor. (Deuteronomy 5:21)

Since you can only covet that which belongs to another, said the rabbis, your neighbor's wife is his personal property. He owns her. In the eyes of the law she is no different from his house, servant or donkey.

Of course, this is not what the tenth commandment is saying, and such a grotesque interpretation conflicts with the other commandments. How can you honor your mother as per the fifth commandment if you value her no more than a donkey?

Moses said that the punishment for adulterers was the same as for adulteresses, but by the time of Jesus, only women were being dragged into the street.

Why did the rabbis of Jesus' day interpret the law in a manner prejudicial to women? They had drunk the Aristotelian Kool-Aid. Some of the religious leaders were so opposed to women that they were known as the "bruised and bleeding Pharisees." They earned this label because they would shut their eyes whenever they saw a woman in the street and walk into walls or posts, bruising themselves.[13]

Philo of Alexandria (~20BC–~50AD) was a Jewish intellectual who worked hard to integrate Jewish scriptures with Greek philosophy. Like Xenophon, Philo believed that a woman's place was in the home:

Market places, and council chambers, and courts of justice, and large companies and assemblies of numerous crowds, and a life in the open air full of arguments and actions relating to war and peace, are suited to men; but taking care of the house and remaining at home are the proper duties of women…[14]

After Philo came **Josephus** (37–100AD) who said, "A woman is inferior to her husband in all things. Let her therefore be obedient to him."[15] Which may explain why Josephus was married four times.

The earliest equalizers

Like the Greeks, many Jewish thinkers believed men were superior to women. But not all Jewish rabbis bought into the Athenian model. One teacher who maintained a refreshingly positive attitude towards women, was Gamaliel, the mentor of Paul.

In his well-researched book *What Paul Really Said about Women*, John Bristow relays a charming story told by Gamaliel. The story is about an emperor who, after learning about the creation of the world from a Jewish sage, exclaimed, "Your God is a thief. To make a woman he had to steal a rib from Adam." The old sage was speechless. He did not know how to reply to this criticism of God. But when the old man's daughter heard what happened, she went to the emperor and cried, "We demand justice!"

"What for?" asked the emperor.

"Thieves broke into our house last night. They took a silver jug and left a gold one in its place."

"I wish I could have burglars like that," said the emperor laughing.

"Well, that is what God did," said the girl. "He took a mere rib from a man and replaced it with a wife."

This delightful story tells us something about the man who trained the apostle Paul. It provides an intriguing context to Paul's belief that men and women are equally valued in the eyes of God.

But Gamaliel and Paul were in the minority, and it's fair to say that the prevailing culture of first-century Israel was prejudicial towards women. The tragedy is how this sexist mindset came to shape the views of Christendom, as we will see in Chapter 6.

After 2,000 years, old stereotypes still exist partly because the church continues to peddle them. "Women are equal, but men are more equal. Women can speak, but not from the pulpit. A woman should not work; her place is in the home." These prejudicial mindsets have impoverished us all. Women who might have changed the world have been held back. Women who might have uttered the words of God have been silenced. God made Eve a queen, but her daughters became servants to men who treated them like chattels and worse.

Now that we know the source of the problem, how do we fix it? Some say we need legislation to right these wrongs. We need to rewrite denominational guidelines and amend church doctrines. But new laws won't change old mindsets. Laws curb sin but leave the heart unaffected. What we need is a fresh revelation of God's purposes for humanity.

Enter Jesus.

4. God's Gift to Women

Jesus began his earthly ministry by listening to a woman. The woman was his mother Mary and all she said was five words: "They have no more wine." Mary and Jesus were at a wedding and their hosts had run out of wine. Mary knew that her son could do something about it.

At first, Jesus seemed reluctant to help. "Woman, why do you involve me? My hour has not yet come." But Mary turned to the servants with a smile and said, "Do whatever he says." Jesus told the servants to fill some jars with water, wine came out, and that was the first time Jesus publicly revealed his glory.[1]

It's a great story. But if all you see is the wine and the wedding, you have missed the significance of the woman.

Look again at how Jesus responds to Mary. He does not say, "I was already planning to make wine," for that would diminish Mary's part in the story. Instead, he chooses words that draw attention to both her lowly status and influence. He calls her woman, tells her this is not the right time, and *then he does what she suggests.* We are left with the impression that the miracle at Cana was entirely her idea.

Jesus was essentially saying, "Woman, because you said it, I'm going to do it." And this at a time when men did not listen to women.

This is some start to the Son of God's ministry!

Do you see? By choosing to reveal himself in response to her words, the Son of God effectively made Mary a partner in his ministry. He heeded her. He followed her lead. Then he made sure that John recorded the story so that we would never forget it.

Eight ways Jesus empowered women

By the time Jesus walked the earth, gender inequality was so entrenched in Jewish society that an adulteress could be stoned without trial and men could divorce their wives for virtually any reason. In a nation of God-fearing and moral men, women were considered little more than property. They were servants whose place was in the kitchen or the field. Some of the religious leaders taught that women were ignorant, yet there was no point teaching them because they had weak minds. Since women were untrustworthy chatterboxes, their testimony had little value in a court of law.

Then along came Jesus.

Jesus encountered all sorts of women, good and bad. Yet unlike the rabbis and the Athenians, he never diminished their humanity. Instead, he treated them with respect and kindness. By including women in all that he did, Jesus provided us with a prophetic picture of the kingdom come. He showed us the world as it was always meant to be. As Gene Edwards has said, "To see how Jesus treated women is to understand what God thinks of women."[2]

Jesus refused to conform to the patriarchal practices of his day. Instead, he empowered and elevated women, and he did this in at least eight ways:

1. Jesus welcomed women

In first-century Israel, women could not enter the best parts of the temple, and they had to sit apart in the synagogue. This religious segregation conveyed an unholy message: when it comes to God, men get preferential treatment. If women wanted to approach God, they needed a male priest to show the way. No man, no God.

Then Jesus came preaching a message of unrestricted access and inviting all to draw near. "Come to me, all who are weary and heavy-laden, and I will give you rest."[3] The Law of Moses specified that only certain men from a certain tribe with certain characteristics could minister to the Lord, but Jesus received all who came to him, whether male or female, young or old. "Whoever comes to me I will never drive away."[4]

What about those who didn't come to him? Jesus went to them.

He went to Samaria to chat with a disreputable woman. He went to Bethany to spend time with Mary and Martha. He even preached in the Women's Court at the Temple (see Box 4.1: The radical geography of Jesus' preaching).

Box 4.1: The radical geography of Jesus' preaching

The temple of Jerusalem was divided into courts. The inner court was called the Court of Israel, the outer court was the Court of Gentiles, and separating these two courts was the Court of the Women. As these names suggest, anyone could walk in the outer court, but only Jewish men could enter the inner court. In which courts did Jesus teach? All of them.[5]

When Jesus sat outside the treasury making remarks about widows and their mites,[6] he was sitting in the Women's Court, because that's where the treasury was located. When he debated with the Pharisees and religious leaders, he was in the Court of Israel, because that's where religious men hung out. When Jesus overturned the tables, he was in the Court of the Gentiles, because that's where the money changers and sacrificial animals were kept.

Jesus preached radical acceptance, and he preached it in radical places. The religious leaders never taught in the Courts of the Gentiles and Women, but Jesus did because he wanted everyone to know how much God loves us.

Before Jesus, the message for women was, "You are not worthy, stay back." But Jesus proclaimed a better message: "Your heavenly Father loves you, draw near." It was the dawn of a new day for the disenfranchised daughters of Eve.

2. Jesus talked to women

In biblical times, women were not supposed to talk to men who weren't their husbands. It was a bad look, suggestive of an inappropriate relationship. The Jewish sages discouraged women from talking to men ("you'll look like an adulterer") and they warned men against talking to women ("you'll go to hell").

Yes, the religious teachers actually said you could burn in hell for talking to a woman.[7]

The disciples, like all good Jewish men, would have been reluctant to speak to women under any circumstances. But Jesus was different. He ignored the rabbis and their rules and spoke to any woman who would speak to him. When women encountered him in the streets, he didn't close his eyes and walk into lampposts like the bloodied and bruised Pharisees. He made time for them and conversed with them. And not just Jewish women. Jesus also spoke to foreign women, unclean women, sinful women—even a woman caught in the act of adultery.

Surely the Jews had never seen a man like this man.

Jesus not only spoke to women; he physically touched them and befriended them.

His affection for Mary and Martha was no secret. When the woman with the alabaster jar poured perfume over his feet, he didn't recoil at her touch but allowed her to minister to him. Then he praised her for doing so.[8]

On one occasion, Jesus was teaching in a synagogue when he saw a woman who had been bent double for eighteen years. This woman would have been sitting with the other women behind a *mechitzah* or divider, but the Son of God fixed his gaze upon her and encouraged her to step out from the manmade barrier.

"Woman, come."

Two words. Yet they tumbled from his mouth like wrecking balls demolishing the citadel of segregation. The broken woman heard her Savior's call, came forward and received her healing.[9]

3. Jesus defended women

After the crippled woman was healed, she found her voice and began praising God. Long years of bondage had come to an end! By the grace of God she was whole! I like to think that Jesus led the assembly in joyous celebration. Perhaps he took the woman by the hand and danced with her. Heaven had come to earth!

But the synagogue ruler was offended by this Jesus who spoke to women and healed on the Sabbath. Nor did he appreciate hearing a woman's voice in his synagogue. "There are six days for work, so come and be healed on those days and not the Sabbath." His rebuke killed the party. The woman stopped dancing. Her friends resumed their seats.

But Jesus wasn't having a bar of it. He got in the man's face and accused him of the worst thing religious men can be accused of. "You hypocrites! Don't you untie your donkeys and lead them to water on the Sabbath? Is that not work?" The ruler wanted to put the woman back behind the barrier, but Jesus fought to keep her free.

In another synagogue, Jesus said, "The Spirit of the Lord is on me to set the oppressed free,"[10] and who is more oppressed than a woman living in a man's world? "I've come to demolish those traditions that silence women," Jesus might've said. "I've come to call women out from whatever barriers are holding them back."

Whenever Jesus encountered women who were being bullied or oppressed, he stood up for them. He warned people against looking at women with lustful eyes. He put himself between the angry mob and the woman caught in adultery. He defended the disreputable woman who anointed him with perfume. When the woman with the issue of blood violated the rules regarding ceremonial cleanness, Jesus did not condemn her for her ritual impurity. He called her daughter and sent her away in peace.[11]

Long before medieval knights developed their chivalric code, Jesus showed men how to defend and speak up for women. The Son of Man was the original champion of women.

4. Jesus opposed wife-dumping

In the patriarchal culture of ancient Israel, there was a law that said a man could divorce his wife if she no longer found favor in his eyes.[12] If she got old and wrinkled, he could trade her in for a younger model. By the time of Jesus, the rabbis and sages had added a raft of other reasons for divorcing your wife. You could divorce her if she spoke with a loud voice, fed you untithed meat, or talked to men in public. If she didn't produce children within ten years, you could divorce her for breaking the commandment to be fruitful and multiply. If she went to a friend's feast after you told her not to, you could divorce her for that too.[13]

These laws were unfair to women and Jesus hated them.

> Jesus replied, "Moses permitted you to divorce your wives because your hearts were hard. But it was not this way from the beginning. I tell you that anyone who divorces his wife, except for sexual immorality, and marries another woman commits adultery." (Matthew 19:8–9)

The Laws of Moses were being interpreted in a way that was harmful to women. Jesus responded by reminding his listeners that divorce undermines God's plan for partnership. "It was not this way in the beginning." Then he said those who divorced their wives and remarried were committing adultery. Actually, Jesus didn't say that. Not exactly. Let's take a closer look.

> Some Pharisees came and tested him by asking, "Is it lawful for a man to divorce his wife?" "What did Moses command you?" he replied. They said, "Moses permitted a man to write a certificate of divorce and send her away." (Mark 10:2–4)

As the Pharisees correctly stated, a Jewish man who wanted to get rid of his wife had to do two things: first he wrote her a certificate of divorce and then he sent her from his house. The problem was some men were doing the latter but not the former. They were sending their wives out into the cold without giving them a *get* or certificate of divorce. It was a horrible thing to do and the tragedy is it was a common practice. Indeed, wife dumping has left such an enduring stain on Jewish history that the Jews have a special name for a women who is sent away without a *get*. Such a woman is known as an *agunah* or a chained wife.[14] She no longer has a husband to provide for her, but since she is technically still married, she cannot remarry.

This practice of wife dumping was abhorrent to Jesus, and he rebuked the men who did it.

> He said to them, "Whoever shall put away his wife, and marry another, commits adultery against her." (Mark 10:11, AKJV)

The issue was not that divorced men were remarrying; it's that men were acting as though they were divorced when they were still married. Because they were sending their wives away without giving them the proper paperwork, they could not remarry without committing adultery.

Admittedly, it can be hard for non-Jews to grasp these distinctions, and it doesn't help when English Bibles muddle the issue. Look at how Mark 10:11 appears in two translations:

> AKJV: Whoever shall put away his wife, and marry another, commits adultery against her.
>
> NIV: Anyone who divorces his wife and marries another woman commits adultery against her.

One Bible says put away; the other says divorce. Which is it? The first one is correct. Jesus was not upset that men were getting divorced but that they were dumping their wives. His concern was for the *agunahs* who were being put or sent away with no means of support.

Why were Jewish men dumping their wives? Perhaps they did it to avoid paying the alimony specified under their marriage contracts.[15] Maybe they were lazy. In any case, it was a wicked thing to do and Jesus called them out. "Whosoever sends away his wife (without a divorce certificate) and marries another, commits adultery."[16] Jesus spoke up for jilted wives by branding their deadbeat husbands law-breakers.

Ouch.

Can you imagine what it was like for a God-fearing Jewish man to be called an adulterer and lawbreaker? By law, an adulterer could be put to death. Jesus had no time for legal mumbo-jumbo, not when women were getting hurt. The rabbis and law-teachers could fish for loopholes, but Jesus spoke plainly: "You're an adulterer, and you're breaking the seventh commandment."

On this issue and many others, Jesus was ahead of his time. Believe it or not, but the problem of wife-dumping was not resolved until 2012. That was the year the Israeli parliament ruled that a husband who wishes to divorce his wife must provide a *get* within 45 days.[17] It only took them 2,000 years to catch up with Jesus.

The practice of wife-dumping was bad enough, but it created another problem that nobody talked about, namely the re-emergence of polygyny.

5. Jesus opposed polygyny

One of the consequences of rebelling against God's partnership plan was the perverted practice of taking more than one wife at a time. Polygyny was practiced in many primitive cultures and is still practiced today in parts of Africa, some Muslim societies, and within the Mormon community. Polygyny was practiced by European Jews until around 1000AD, but it was not made illegal in Israel until 1977. Nevertheless, polygyny is still practiced today by Jews in Islamic countries as well as Bedouin and Orthodox Jews in Israel.[18]

Were the Jews of Jesus' day polygynous? For the most part, they were moral and monogamous. Unlike the ancients, they knew that a man should have only one wife. But because of their cynical exploitation of the divorce laws, some married men were remarrying and becoming bigamists. This was the one of the scandals of Jewish society, and Jesus publicly opposed it.

When some Pharisees questioned Jesus on the subject of divorce, he responded by reminding them of God's original plan for partnership:

> But at the beginning of creation God "made them male and female." "For this reason a man will leave his father and mother and be united to his wife, and the two will become one flesh." So they are no longer two, but one flesh. Therefore what God has joined together, let no one separate. (Mark 10:6–9)

Notice how Jesus emphasizes the number two: "The *two* shall become one flesh; they are no longer *two*." A marriage has two people, not three or four. Put it all together, and Jesus is saying something like this:

> You argue about divorce, but some of you have multiple wives! Do you think God is fooled by your hypocrisy and poor treatment of women?

Polygyny may not be a big deal today, but our ignorance of these matters has caused some to say that women can't lead. "An elder must be a husband of one wife, therefore women can't serve in ministry." This is based on something Paul said in his letters to Timothy and Titus, but Paul was not saying women can't be elders or deacons. He was saying men who are unfaithful with their own brides cannot be trusted with the bride of Christ. We will take a closer look at Paul's words in Part B, but the short version is, he was speaking against polygyny, just as Jesus did.

6. Jesus told stories about women

In the male-dominated world of the Bible, women were largely invisible. They were non-speaking extras on the stage of humanity.

51

Men had the major roles; women had bit parts. However, Jesus challenged the marginalization of women by making them the central players in his parables.

In one parable, Jesus compared the kingdom of heaven to the yeast a woman works into her dough. In another parable, the heavenly rejoicing over repentant sinners is compared to the joy of a woman finding a misplaced coin. In the parable of the wise and foolish virgins, women have most of the speaking parts. But Jesus' most remarkable parable, in terms of elevating women, is surely the one about the persistent widow.[19]

This widow was a remarkable woman. She had no rights and no power, yet she frightened an unjust judge into doing his job. Bothered by her frequent visits, the crooked judge said to himself, "This widow won't quit badgering me. I'd better see that she gets justice; otherwise I'm going to end up beaten black and blue by her pounding."[20]

How can a weak widow unnerve a fearless and powerful judge? The picture is so incomprehensible that some Bible translations dilute her actions. They say she will wear out the judge, perhaps with her ceaseless nagging. But that's not what Jesus said. He said the judge feared that the widow would assault him. She was going to punch him on the nose. And why not? He surely deserves it.

Women cheered when they heard this story. They knew the bitter injustice of living in a world where men have all the power. There would have had been occasions when they wanted to thump some officious blockhead who had mistreated them. Of course, they could do no such thing, which is why the women in Jesus' stories were so inspiring.

Instead of reinforcing patriarchal norms marginalizing women, Jesus told stories of justice and equality. He spoke of the daughters of Abraham as often as he spoke of Abraham's sons. And when casting about for a metaphor for how he felt towards the recalcitrant people of Jerusalem, he compared himself to a mother hen gathering her chicks.[21] No rabbi would have compared the Messiah to a female hen, but Jesus was no mere rabbi. He was the Son of the One who made both men and women in his glorious image.

7. Jesus discipled women

One of the most revolutionary ways Jesus empowered women was by accepting them as his disciples. He welcomed them into his circle and trained them, something that would have been unthinkable to the rabbis and sages. Teaching women was a waste of time, said Rabbi Eliezer. "It would be better to burn the words of the law than teach them to women."[22]

Every educated man knew that women were mentally deficient. They could learn to cook and spin wool, but that was the limit of their abilities. Women belonged in the kitchen, and this is why Mary's departure from that room ought to be hailed as a seminal moment in the history of women's liberation.

Mary of Bethany crossed an ancient line. She stepped across the threshold, entered the front room where the men normally sat, and placed herself at the feet of Jesus, *like a disciple*. Any other rabbi would have blanched and waited for her to leave. But Jesus welcomed her with a smile and commended her courageous act. Then he encouraged Martha to follow her sister's example.[23]

Something we may not appreciate is just how many women followed Jesus. Paintings of our Lord teaching typically show him surrounded by men. If women are depicted, they are usually in the minority or hidden in the background. But when Jesus hung on the cross, the men fled while "many women" remained.[24] Who were these women who stood by the Lord in his darkest hour? They were his disciples.

After this, Jesus travelled about from one town and village to another, proclaiming the good news of the kingdom of God. The Twelve were with him, and also some women... (Luke 8:1–2a)

Box 4.2: Jesus, the pioneer of women's education

In many countries today, women can enroll in higher education, but it was not always this way. Women did not begin studying at university in Britain until 1869. In the US, the first college to admit women was Oberlin College, in 1837. The University of Bologna in Italy was reputedly the first in the world to accept women, which it started doing in the 13th century. In the history of women's education, these are significant milestones. Yet Jesus, the original discipler of women, beat them all by more than a thousand years.

In the history of education, one trailblazing group that appears again and again are Christian missionaries and reformers. In many countries, Christians were the first to teach women and girls. Long before American colleges began admitting women for degrees, seminaries, such as the Bethlehem Female Seminary in Pennsylvania, or Salem College in North Carolina, were providing women with opportunities for higher education.[25] In the 19th century, pioneers like the English philosopher John Stuart Mill and the American preachers Charles Finney and D.L. Moody promoted the education of women long before such ideas were accepted by the wider public.

If women enjoy equal educational opportunities today, it's because Jesus and those who followed him refused to conform to a sexist system that denied women the right to learn.

Wherever Jesus went, men and women followed. This was highly unusual. In those days, women didn't follow men who weren't their husbands, but they followed Jesus.

"Whoever wants to be my disciple must deny themselves and take up their cross daily and follow me."[26] When Jesus outlined the qualifications of a disciple, he made no restrictions for gender. Again, this was unprecedented. Although Socrates and a few others made noises about educating women, Jesus actually did it (see Box 4.2: Jesus, the pioneer of women's education). He took them on as disciples and trained them.

On another occasion, Jesus asked,

"Who is my mother, and who are my brothers?" Pointing to his disciples, he said, "Here are my mother and my brothers. For whoever does the will of my Father in heaven is my brother and sister and mother." (Matthew 12:48–50)

Jesus did not point at Peter and John and call them his mother and sister. Clearly, there were women among his disciples. Tradition teaches that the women in his group were little more than hangers-on. They were there because they had money or because Jesus was too kind to send them away. They weren't real disciples. Nothing could be further from the truth.

Some of Jesus' most famous teachings were uttered exclusively to women. Jesus told Martha he was the resurrection and the life. He preached the message of no condemnation to the woman caught in adultery. He discussed the meaning of true worship with the woman at the well, and his first Gentile convert was a Syrophoenician woman. Most famously of all, he first revealed the good news of his resurrection to a group of women.

It's as if Jesus saved his best stuff for his female followers.

This was no accident. Jesus was modeling something the world had never seen—a church where women served alongside men as equal partners in the gospel.

8. Jesus commissioned women to preach the good news

On a hot afternoon in Samaria, Jesus met a woman by a well and told her that he was the Messiah she was waiting for. The woman was so transformed by her encounter with the Lord that she left her water jar and became an evangelist. What happened next was unprecedented. "Many of the Samaritans from that town believed *because of the woman's testimony.*"[27]

And this when a woman's testimony wasn't worth spit.

If Jesus had been more in tune with the masculine norms of the day, he would have called her back. "Wait, I can't build my church with women preachers! What was I thinking? I'll send one of the boys." But Jesus said nothing of the sort, and the woman made history. Then one of Jesus' disciples recorded her story in his gospel so that we might be inspired by her example.

After Jesus rose from the dead, he appeared to three women. They were Mary Magdalene, Joanna, and Mary, the mother of James. In Matthew's account of the story, the women were running to tell the disciples that the tomb was empty when Jesus met them on the way. "Do not be afraid," he said. "Go and tell my brothers to go to Galilee where they will see me."[28]

Which begs the question, why didn't Jesus tell the disciples himself?

Peter and John came to the tomb as well, but the Risen Lord did not reveal himself to them. He announced his risenness to women and instructed them to go and tell the others.

Go and tell. Is this not the essence of the Great Commission? All followers of Christ are exhorted to tell the good news that Christ is risen, but the first to be called were women.

Evidently, Jesus wasn't opposed to women preachers.

Jesus began his earthly ministry by listening to a woman, and he concluded it by conversing with more women. In between these conversations, Jesus spent a great deal of time engaging with women. He treated women with respect, he defended them against bullies, and he trained them to be fully-fledged partners in his ministry.

Before Jesus no one treated women like this. Because of Jesus, the world would never be the same.

We have looked at eight ways Jesus empowered women, and to be fair, most of them would not be considered radical in the modern church. Most Christians would agree that it's fine for men to talk to women in public, just as it's normal for women to be educated and call themselves followers of Christ. But where some draw the line is with the suggestion that women can teach and preach and lead men to Jesus.

"Jesus appointed twelve Jewish men to represent him, proving that women cannot lead in the church." By the same logic, it also proves that only Jewish men can preach and pastor. Of course it proves no such thing. If a pastor can be an American or an Australian, a pastor can be a woman.

But why did Jesus choose twelve men? It's a fair question that deserves a proper answer (see Box 4.3: Why didn't Jesus appoint female apostles?). Here is another good question: What did those twelve men think of women? Did they partner with them in the ministry? Did they let them preach and teach? It is to these questions that we now turn.

Box 4.3: Why didn't Jesus appoint female apostles?

Jesus did not choose male apostles because he was sexist, but because his listeners were. The first-century Jews would never have listened to women in the same way they listened to Peter and John. Their prejudice against women was noted by Josephus: "Let not the testimony of women be admitted, on account of the levity and boldness of their sex."[29]

In other words, you can't trust a woman.

Jesus instructed his apostles to be his witnesses first in Jerusalem and Judea.[30] That could only work if the witnesses were Jewish men because Jewish men wouldn't listen to anybody else. Thus we find Peter addressing the crowd of Jewish pilgrims in Acts 2, and then Peter and John preaching together in Acts 3 and 4. Later we see Stephen, another Jewish man, preaching to the Sanhedrin in Acts 7, before Paul addresses the same group later in the book. Horses for courses.

When the gospel spread beyond sexist Judea, women began to play a more prominent role in preaching it, as we shall see in the next chapter.

5. What Did the Apostles Think about Women in Ministry?

In the Garden, God revealed his plan for partnership, and in the Gospels, Jesus put that plan into action. But what did the apostles do? Did they buy into the partnership model and treat women as equals? Or did they revert to the old ways of patriarchy?

After Jesus ascended into heaven, the eleven remaining apostles, "along with the women," devoted themselves to prayer.[1] This was the first hint that the New Testament church would follow the pattern modeled by Jesus. A church prayer meeting might not strike us as particularly historic, but the first one represented an astounding leap forward for women's rights. Men and women were praying together. The women were not sitting behind a divider, and the men were not shutting their ears to the prayers of women.

In Acts 2, the believers were together in one place when there was a noise from heaven like the roar of a mighty wind. Tongues of fire came to rest on each of them, and they were filled with the Holy Spirit. All of the disciples, both male and female, began speaking in tongues. A crowd gathered to watch the spectacle. No one had ever seen such a thing. What did it mean? Peter stood up and gave this explanation:

> In the last days, God says, I will pour out my Spirit on all people. Your sons *and daughters* will prophesy... Even on my servants, both men *and women*, I will pour out my Spirit in those days, and they will prophesy. (Acts 2:17–18)

God was bringing change, said Peter. Women were to remain silent and hidden no longer. From now on, they would be treated as equal partners in the ministry of the Holy Spirit.

Jesus had shown the way, and on the Day of Pentecost the new church embraced God's plan for partnership. The results were instant and dramatic. Within a short time, thousands of Judean men and women had turned to God. In neighboring Samaria, Philip was baptizing both men and women. Even priests, those purveyors of patriarchy, were coming to Jesus.[2]

More spirited than lions

Perhaps the most dramatic sign of women's participation in the new church was this: a Pharisee called Saul began throwing them in prison.

> But Saul began to destroy the church. Going from house to house, he dragged off both men *and women* and put them in prison. (Acts 8:3)

Prior to Pentecost, women were never arrested. They never did anything. On the night Jesus was crucified, the male disciples fled in fear, but his female followers lingered at the cross untroubled. Since they were no threat to the religious leaders, they had no reason to flee. But by the time of Saul, Christian women had become active partners in the gospel. Consequently, they were rounded up and imprisoned along with the men.

> Meanwhile, Saul was still breathing out murderous threats against the Lord's disciples. He went to the high priest and asked him for letters to the synagogues in Damascus, so that if he found any there who belonged to the Way, whether men *or women*, he might take them as prisoners to Jerusalem. (Acts 9:1–2)

Saul was an equal-opportunities persecutor. Years later, he would say he had "persecuted this Way to death" and was responsible for putting "both men and women into prisons."[3] In those days, people did not go to prison to serve long sentences but to await trial. It's reasonable to conclude that Saul, who later became Paul, was responsible for the murder of Christian men and women.

Why kill women? There is only one explanation. After Jesus, women found their voice. After Pentecost, women stepped up, and those who became partners in ministry became partners in martyrdom.

"What women these Christians have!" exclaimed the fourth-century Greek rhetorician Libanius. He was not a believer, but his pupil, John Chrysostom, became the Archbishop of Constantinople. This is what Chrysostom said about the women of the early church:

> The women of those days were more spirited than lions, sharing with the Apostles their labors for the Gospel's sake. In this way they went travelling with them, and also performed all other ministries.[4]

Who were these women? We will meet some of them later in this book. But for now, let us pay a visit to the church of Rome where we will encounter some exceptional women.

The praiseworthy women of Rome

In the final chapter of his letter to the Romans, Paul identifies 29 people. Some of these people he greets, while others receive special acknowledgment and praise. If we divide the 29 Romans into two groups—those Paul merely greets versus those he praises—we discover some interesting patterns. For instance, women make up only 30 percent of the names on Paul's list, yet they receive more than 60 percent of his apostolic high-fives. Of the men that Paul identifies, 74 percent are merely greeted. In contrast, 80 percent of the women are praised.

The women in the Roman church were not second-tier Christians beholden to the male leaders. In Paul's eyes, they had an equal stake in the church, and they were doing praiseworthy work. Since Paul praises more women than men, we might even conclude that the women of Rome were doing the lion's share of the ministry.

Greet Mary, who worked very hard for you... Greet Tryphena and Tryphosa, those women who work hard in the Lord. Greet my dear friend Persis, another woman who has worked very hard in the Lord. (Romans 16:6, 12)

Paul names four women who worked hard in the Lord. What sort of work did they do? They did the same work that Paul did, which was preach and teach the gospel. They were ministers of the gospel. Why else would Paul praise their labors?

No one else in scripture acknowledged the ministry of women to the degree that Paul did, and this is fitting. Paul, the former persecutor of Christian women, understood better than anyone God's plan for men and women to work together.

Gender roles in the new creation

It's true that some of the scriptures penned by Paul have been misused to oppress women, and we'll get to those in Part B. But Paul was actively opposed to discrimination of any kind. He never treated women as second-class or inferior. Instead, he made counter-cultural pronouncements like this:

There is neither Jew nor Gentile, neither slave nor free, nor is there male and female, for you are all one in Christ Jesus. (Galatians 3:28)

Male privilege has no place in the new creation. All people, regardless of race, status, or gender, are equally valued in the family of God. Although men and women are biologically different, they are equal in grace. This has enormous implications for our view of women and their role in the church. Can women preach and lead and do all the things men do? If they are equal partners, why not?

Yet some disagree. They say that Galatians 3:28 pertains to salvation only. "Anyone can come to Christ to be saved, but not everyone can preach and pastor." This interpretation seems to fit the context because Paul is talking about how we are justified by faith. "You are all sons of God through faith in Christ Jesus."[5] Yet the notion that some in Christ have advantages over others would have appalled Paul. In Christ, there are no second-class citizens. We are all sons of God. Even the daughters.

Others say, "Equal value does not mean equal role. Women are equally important as men, but they can't do the same things as men." It is true that within the body of Christ, different members perform different functions. But our role is determined by our calling, not our gender, and those who have been qualified by God should not be disqualified by men.

> We have different gifts, according to the grace given to each of us. If your gift is prophesying, then prophesy in accordance with your faith; if it is serving, then serve; if it is teaching, then teach; if it is to encourage, then give encouragement; if it is giving, then give generously; if it is to lead, do it diligently; if it is to show mercy, do it cheerfully. (Romans 12:6–8)

Paul wrote these words to a church full of active women. Maybe they were active because Paul had encouraged them to operate in their God-given gifts and callings. Among the apostles, there was no greater encourager of women, except maybe Peter, who wrote this:

> Each of you should use whatever gift you have received to serve others, as faithful stewards of God's grace in its various forms. If anyone speaks, they should do so as one who speaks the very words of God. (1 Peter 4:10–11a)

As a Jewish man, Peter had been raised under the old law-keeping covenant. The old covenant was racist (Jews are special) and sexist (men are privileged), but the new covenant is neither.

After being with Jesus, Peter understood that gender distinctions were irrelevant to the ministry of the Spirit. Notice the absence of qualifiers in his words. Peter does not say the gift of speaking is only for men and that women must remain silent. He says, "each of you" and "if anyone." If God has gifted you to speak, then speak as though speaking the very words of God, and let no one silence you.

Peter and Paul make an intriguing tag team. While the former was encouraging women to speak up, the latter was arresting them for doing so. Then Paul saw the light and began singing from the same songbook. Like Peter, Paul believed in the *koinonia*-partnership of all believers. He understood that the body of Christ needs every part—male and female—to function properly:

> The head cannot say to the feet, "I don't need you!" … there should be no division in the body, but that its parts should have equal concern for each other. If one part suffers, every part suffers with it; if one part is honored, every part rejoices with it. Now you are the body of Christ, and each one of you is a part of it. (1 Corinthians 12:21, 25–27)

How do we practice *koinonia*? By having equal concern for one another and by recognizing the gifts God has given to each other. And how do we sabotage *koinonia*? By telling women they don't have the same rights and opportunities as men.

What about the other apostles?

Peter and Paul were not the only apostles to support women in the early church. There were at least four others. Their names were Matthew, Mark, Luke and John. The contributions of these four courageous men cannot be overstated. They literally wrote women back into the history books.

The women in the Old Testament were mostly silent and anonymous. Once every few hundred years or so, a woman spoke loud enough to get noticed by the men writing the Bible, but for the most part, the women of old were nonspeaking extras on the stage of humanity. But as soon as we get to the Gospels, it's like women suddenly found their voice.

Or rather, men started listening.

The four Gospel writers filled their books with the words and deeds of women. Unlike the writers who came before them and many who came after, they made women look good. They gave them a voice and acknowledged their contribution to the human story.

What is remarkable is how each writer opens his Gospel with a womanly tale, as if to set the scene for all that follows. In the early pages of John's Gospel, we hear Mary telling Jesus to reveal his true nature. Luke begins his Gospel with Mary and Elizabeth marveling at the imminent arrival of the Messiah. In the first chapter of Mark, we learn how Jesus physically touched and healed a sick woman. These were scandalous stories, but the one told by Matthew takes the cake.

Like any good Jewish biographer, Matthew begins by outlining Jesus' family tree. "Abraham begat Isaac, and Isaac begat Jacob, and so forth." But then Matthew makes the startling announcement that Jesus' mother was unmarried at the time of her pregnancy. "Mary was pledged to be married to Joseph, but before they came together, she was found to be pregnant through the Holy Spirit."[6] In the eyes of the religious teachers, how could Mary be anything but a fornicator? She was no such thing, insisted Matthew. She was the virginal mother of our Messiah, as foretold by prophecy.

The human race is divided over the story of the virgin birth, yet Matthew did not hesitate to stake his reputation on the story.

If Matthew, Mark, Luke, and John had been cut from the same cloth as the Jewish rabbis or the Greek philosophers, they would not have included all those stories about Jesus talking to women and befriending them. They would not have mentioned that Jesus had female disciples or that he sent women to proclaim the good news. But these four men had heard the roar of the Lord. They understood God's heart for humanity and his plan for partnership. So they elevated women and became leaders in a revolution that continues to this day.

Box 5.1: The new normal of the New Testament

On the night Jesus rose from the dead, two of his followers were walking to Emmaus when they encountered the risen Lord. Not recognizing their fellow traveler, they proceeded to update him regarding Jesus' recent crucifixion and his resurrection. The disciples said that "certain women of our company" had discovered an empty tomb that very morning. "They came and told us they had seen a vision of angels, who said he was alive."[7]

With this short exchange we witness the beginnings of a profound shift in the male mindset. These men did not care that women were regarded as unreliable witnesses or that men weren't supposed to talk to women. Nor did they care that their company included female disciples. The world was different now. Because Jesus valued women, they valued women. Because Jesus spoke to women, they spoke to women.

For the men who had been with Jesus, everything had changed. Treating women with respect had become the new normal, and it stayed normal all through the New Testament.

Many of us have inherited our views on women from unscriptural traditions invented by men. Perhaps it is time for us to challenge those views. The question we need to ask is not what does my church teach about women, but what did the New Testament church teach? As we have seen, those who had been with Jesus were fully committed to the Lord's partnership plan. In the early church, men and women served side by side and as a result the Gospel bore fruit all over the world.

Did it last? What happened when the men and women who had been with Jesus passed on? Did those who followed them stay the course?

6. What Did the Church Fathers Think about Women?

In World War Two, 166 women got to experience a level of freedom and equality that few women had experienced before. They were the brave women of England's Air Transport Auxiliary or ATA. Known as Attagirls, these women delivered new and repaired warplanes to air bases. They didn't engage in combat, but they played a critical role in keeping squadrons supplied with Spitfires, Hurricanes, and every other type of aircraft.

In the beginning, the ATA employed only male pilots. But as the needs of the war effort grew, women fliers fought for and won the right to fly planes. Initially, women were only allowed to fly non-combat types of aircraft such as trainers and transport. Eventually, they were permitted to fly fighters and heavy bombers as well. These women were capable fliers. One pilot, Mary Ellis (nee Wilkins), flew an estimated 76 types of aircraft, including 400 different Spitfires.[1]

The recruitment of women fliers in 1940 was not without opposition. In 1941, the editor of *Aeroplane Magazine* wrote:

> We quite agree that there are millions of women in the country who could do useful jobs in war. But the trouble is that so many insist on wanting to do jobs which they are quite incapable of doing. The menace is the woman who thinks she ought to be flying a high speed bomber when she really has not the intelligence to scrub the floor of a hospital properly.[2]

Despite these objections, the demands of the war outweighed all other concerns, and from 1943 to 1945, these women fliers were treated as equal to men in all respects. They faced the same risks, they lost their lives, and they received commendations. They even earned the same pay and held command positions over men.[3] Then the war ended, their jobs disappeared, and they were expected to resume their pre-war roles as supportive wives. For experienced fliers such as Joy Lofthouse, the reversal came as an unpleasant shock:

To be perfectly honest, I wanted the war to go on as long as possible. Wartime gave many women something they'd never had: independence, earning your own money, being your own person. Once you married, everything changed dramatically.[4]

For a brief spell in the mid-1940s, women fliers enjoyed a rare taste of equality. But after the war, they were kicked out of their planes, and inequality reigned for a further 30 years. That's how long it took before Emily Howell Warner and Bonnie Tiburzi became the first women to pilot commercial airliners.[5]

The up and down story of women aviators parallels the story of women in the church. For a hundred years or so following the resurrection of Jesus, Christian women enjoyed equality with men. They preached, pastored, and prophesied and did whatever the men did. However, within a few generations of the original apostles, a new breed of men emerged to reassert male primacy and to lead the church back to patriarchy. These men are known to us as the early Church Fathers, and they gave their name to the so-called Patristic Era.

Who were the Church Fathers? They were ecclesiastical influencers who wrote letters and books on a variety of topics. They were also intellectuals who had been educated in a Hellenistic culture. They read the words of Jesus and the apostles through an Aristotelian lens, and they introduced the thoughts of Socrates, Xenophon, and Plato to a Christian audience.

The Church Fathers, according to some, said many outrageous and vile things about women. However, in my research for this book, I found that some of the worst quotes attributed to these men were fabrications or had been lifted out of context. For example, Jerome of Stridon is dismissed by some as the most misogynistic man to ever darken God's green earth. Again and again I read how Jerome said women were the root of all evil. Only he never said it. Like his contemporaries, Jerome said bizarre things about women, but he also had many female friends and students.

Get your knowledge of history from certain websites and books and you'll come away thinking that the Church Fathers were a bunch of witch hunters. They weren't. You will also alienate yourself from Catholic and Orthodox friends who venerate these men and are better acquainted with history.

I have no desire to besmirch the reputation of the Church Fathers, but if we are to right present wrongs, we must confront our sexist heritage. This heritage was shaped by God-fearing men who, like the philosophers and rabbis before them, viewed women as inferior and subservient. What follows is a brief summary of some of the more extreme claims they made about women.

What did the Church Fathers say about women?

One of the most contentious subjects in the church is the question of what women can wear. Peter and Paul touched on this issue, and so did **Clement** of Alexandria (150–215AD). Clement believed that women should be veiled so that men might not be tempted to sin. "For it is a wicked thing for beauty to be a snare to men." Veils could be any color, said Clement, but definitely not one of those "stupid and luxurious purples" that inflame lust.[6]

Tertullian of Carthage (155–240AD), the father of Latin Christianity, wrote an entire book on *The Apparel of Women*. In it he wonders why women aren't permanently dressed in mourning garments on account of them being the cause of humanity's Fall.

> The sentence of God on this sex of yours lives on even in our times and so it is necessary that the guilt should live on also. You are the one who opened the door to the devil, you are the one who first plucked the fruit of the forbidden tree, you are the first who deserted the divine law; you are the one who persuaded him whom the devil was not strong enough to attack. All too easily you destroyed the image of God, man. Because of your desert, that is, death, even the Son of God had to die.[7]

69

Jerome (347–420) wrote the most influential New Testament of all time, the Latin Vulgate. Jerome is revered by some as a saint, but he held strange views about women and marriage. Jerome was obsessed with virginity and believed marriage was a result of the Fall.[8] He promoted asceticism and said a woman who abstained from sex was as good as a man.[9] He also believed chastity was synonymous with holiness, and he encouraged parents to send their daughters to nunneries.[10]

Augustine (354–430AD), the Bishop of Hippo and a contemporary of Jerome's, said women had low intelligence, were not made in the image of God, and were good for little more than making babies. Women were dangerous, said Augustine, because they carried the genes of that temptress Eve.[11]

Jesus and the apostles encouraged women to speak up and lead, and for 300 years they did. Then in the middle of the fourth century, the **Council of Laodicea** (363–364AD) banned the appointment of women leaders. In his commentary on this prohibition, **Theodore Balsamon**, the 12th-century Eastern Orthodox Patriarch of Antioch, said this:

> For woman to teach in a Catholic Church, where a multitude of men is gathered together, and women of different opinions, is, in the highest degree, indecorous and pernicious.[12]

Among Catholics, there may be no greater theologian than **Thomas Aquinas** (1225–1274). Yet Aquinas said women were created in the image of man and not God, and that "man is the beginning and end of woman, as God is the beginning and end of every creature."[13] And what made women inferior? Women were "defective and misbegotten," explained the learned theologian, because they were conceived on wet and windy days.[14]

You can't make this stuff up.

The great reformer **Martin Luther** (1483–1546) believed in the priesthood of all believers, but only if they were men. Women have weaker minds and were "chiefly created to bear children, and be the pleasure, joy, and solace of their husbands."[15]

Luther did not think that women were as bad as others said, but he certainly thought that men were better.

> For as the sun is more glorious than the moon, though the moon is a most glorious body, so woman, though she was a most beautiful work of God, yet she did not equal the glory of the male creature.[16]

However, Luther also said that before the Fall of Man, Eve was in no respect inferior to Adam. Any subjection to man was the result of sin and not part of God's original design.

> Had Eve therefore stood in the truth she would not only have been free from all subjection to the rule of the man, but she herself also would have been an equal partaker of government, which now belongs to men alone.[17]

The French reformer **John Calvin** (1509–1564) disagreed. Calvin said the subjection of women to the authority of men reflected God's eternal law.[18] It was never God's plan to create two chiefs of equal power, but one chief and an inferior aid.[19] Consequently, "It is the dictate of common sense, that female government is improper and unseemly."[20]

I said earlier that the Church Fathers were not witch hunters. However, one man who did hunt witches was **King James I** (1566–1625) of England. King James, of course, is known to us for the Bible he commissioned. What is less well known is how James was staunchly opposed to women. In 1597, he authored a tract called *Daemonologie* in which he advocated the execution of women convicted of witchcraft. The English king was obsessed with witchcraft, and he personally supervised the torture of women accused of being witches.

Box 6.1: Is the King James Bible sexist?

The King James Version has been called the most influential book in the world. A literary masterpiece, it introduced into the English language some of our most beautiful words and most memorable aphorisms. But like any Bible translation, it reflects the culture and theology of those who translated it. Which is why the 400 year old KJV, and some of the translations that followed it, seems to exhibit a subtle bias against women.

Some examples: In Acts, the order of Priscilla and Aquila's names is arbitrarily reversed with the husband listed first.[21] Paul said a woman should learn in quietness, but the KJV says a woman should learn in silence.[22] When Paul introduced Phoebe to the Romans, he called her a deacon, but the KJV introduces her as a servant.[23] The KJV turns Euodia, a female co-worker named by Paul, into a man: Euodias.[24]

One of the more blatant examples of sexist language is found in the qualifications for elders and deacons found in Paul's first letter to Timothy. Paul used gender-neutral language: "Anyone who desires the office of bishop desires a good work." However, the KJV translators replaced Paul's words with gender-specific words: "If a man desire the office of a Bishop, he desireth a good work." Paul said *anyone* may desire the office, but the KJV says *any man* giving the impression that only men can lead.

When King James issued his translators with instructions, he told them to follow existing Bibles as closely as possible. Why does the 17th-century KJV say any man in 1 Timothy 3:1? Because every 16th-century English Bible says it, including the Miles Coverdale Bible (1535), the Great Bible (1539), the Bishops Bible (1568), and the Geneva Bible (1599). This suggests that the translators were either masculinizing scripture in a way that was consistent with cultural norms, or they understood that *any man* meant *any one*. In any case, our failure to understand these distinctions can lead to sexist conclusions that were never intended by Paul.

Our tarnished heritage

Jesus and the apostles were fearless revolutionaries who defied longstanding prejudices by fighting for the emancipation of women. In contrast, some of the Church Fathers who followed them were mealy-mouthed conformists who merely parroted what they had learned in school. They saw themselves as God's men preaching God's word, but their beliefs about women came straight out of Greece.

Xenophon the philosopher told his fifteen-year-old wife, "God has assigned women the indoor tasks," and the Church Fathers said a hearty "Amen!"[25] Aristotle said bad men would be resurrected as women, and Thomas Aquinas added that good women would be raised as men.[26] Hesiod said women were tricksters out to ruin men, while Augustine said they were temptresses in the mold of Eve. If you have ever wondered why the modern church treats women like second-class citizens, you can thank the Church Fathers and the rabbis and philosophers who preceded them.

To be fair, the Church Fathers were hardly the only men who believed women were deficient. Make a list of men who held screwy ideas about women, and you will have to include some of the most famous thinkers and leaders in history, including Kant, Goethe, Schopenhauer, Napoleon, Nietzsche, Kierkegaard, Tolstoy, Freud, Marx and others.[27] But the Church Fathers should have known better. The apostles heard the roar of the Lord, but they didn't. When it came to women, they preferred the bad news of Athens to the good news of the kingdom.

Happily, the world is changing. After many long centuries of injustice, the world is finally starting to line up with God's original plan. In many societies, women can now study, vote, and fly airplanes. They still get paid less for doing more, and they are more likely to get passed over, assaulted, and aborted. But the underlying trend is good. Even the church is starting to shrug off some of its inherited prejudices.

But we have a long way to go if we are to roll back the damage inflicted by our ecclesiastical forebears. For the sake of our wives, our daughters and ourselves, we need to do more and do it faster. One way to hasten the process is to confront our inherited traditions. In Part B, we will turn our attention to those scriptures that have been misused to muzzle and mistreat women.

Part B: Questions and Answers

7. Are Wives Merely Helpmates?

"Women were made to be helpers to men," said Thomas Aquinas, "just as the scripture says."[1] Aquinas was referring to this verse:

The Lord God said, "It is not good for the man to be alone. I will make a helper suitable for him." (Genesis 2:18)

Nearly every commentator will tell you that the intended helper was Eve. The 17th-century English theologian Matthew Poole said God created woman to be a second self to man, "one to be at hand and near to him, to stand continually before him… always ready to succor, serve, and comfort him."[2]

What about Eve's needs for succor and comfort? In the standard text on this passage, the woman's needs are rarely mentioned. Eve is the helper, Adam is the one helped, and this patriarchal pattern is reinforced whenever wives are told to serve their husbands.

Matthew Poole said a wife's primary occupation "shall be to please and help him." In other words, a good wife is like a butler, or a "faithful assistant," to use John Calvin's phrase. Although "men are often disturbed by their wives, and suffer through them many discouragements," said Calvin, we owe it to our wives to let them help us so that we may fulfill our divinely-ordained role as head and leader.[3]

What a guy.

In the next chapter we will ask, "Were women created to serve men?" (Spoiler alert: they weren't.) But for now let us consider what it means to be a helper.

The suitable Helper

There is no question that Eve was an essential part of God's plan for humanity. But why did God delay in making her? Why have a gap between the man and the woman? God made Adam and declared, "It is not good for the man to be alone." If it was not good for man to be alone, why did God make man alone? He did it to help Adam realize his need for partnership.

"I will make a helper suitable for him." God was talking about Eve and marriage and everything that goes with that. A helper is a partner is a helper. But after saying this, God did something unexpected: He gave Adam an impossible assignment.

"Name the animals and birds."

"All of them, Lord?"

"Every last one."

"There are so many. I can't do it."

"I know."

"So how…"

"I will help you," says the Lord, and he does. He rounds up every type of bird and animal and brings them to Adam to be named. God does the hard part, and Adam does the easy part. It's an unusual story, but it illuminates a timeless truth: Without God we can do nothing, but with him we can accomplish great things.

Is this not the key to life? We all need help. Every one of us was born with needs that we cannot meet—needs for love, acceptance, and affirmation. These God-given needs were hardwired into us to lead us to our true Source.

God won't ask you to name all the animals, but chances are he has given you a dream or a mission that is too big for you to handle. This God-sized task is written into your members. It's so audacious that it takes your breath away. It seems impossible that you could ever accomplish this Great Big Thing by yourself. And that's the point.

It is not good for any of us to be alone.

Our present Help

A recurring theme in scripture is that God is our present help in times of trouble. The Lord is our Helper who rides across the heavens to help us.[4] Perhaps no one understood the help of God better than the psalmist:

> I lift up my eyes to the mountains—where does my help come from? My help comes from the Lord, the Maker of heaven and earth. (Psalm 121:1–2)

We are weak, but God is powerful, and he wants to help us. In the Old Testament, the supernatural aid of God is linked with many blessings, including strength, protection, deliverance, peace, comfort, and joy. And in the New Testament, we are exhorted to come boldly to God's throne of grace to receive help in time of need.[5]

> So we say with confidence, "The Lord is my helper; I will not be afraid. What can mere mortals do to me?" (Hebrews 13:6)

Throughout scripture, God is identified as *the* Helper.[6] So when God says, "I will make a suitable helper for man," and then follows it up by giving Adam an impossible task that he can only complete with divine aid, could it be that God was alluding to something more than another human? Could it be that God was inviting Adam to see him not as a distant deity, but as a Father who wanted to be involved in his life? "Adam, I want to walk with you, talk with you, and help you."

Did Adam get the message? Apparently not. "But for Adam no suitable helper was found." Adam looked at the birds and the animals. He saw they were in pairs and wondered where his other half was. Instead of looking up, he looked around and saw an empty world.

I can't prove this from scripture, but I believe God's heart broke that day. He created Adam for fellowship, but Adam wasn't interested. God tried to get his attention, but Adam looked away.

The Florentine painter Michelangelo captured Adam's indifference in his Sistine Chapel masterpiece, "The Creation of Adam." In the painting God is straining down from heaven trying to reach

Adam, but a recumbent Adam is leaning away from God, barely extending his arm.

Adam didn't recognize his heavenly Helper. He wanted a copy of himself. He said of Eve, "She shall be called 'woman,' for she was taken out of man."[7] Adam's preferred helper literally came from his own flesh.

Jerry Maguire was wrong

The eponymous lead in the film *Jerry Maguire* told the woman he loved, "You complete me." But it's a mistake to think your life is incomplete without a spouse. Burden your partner with God-sized expectations, and you'll sink your marriage. It is God who makes us whole, heals our hurts, and helps us soar.

Yet the grace of God comes to us through people, including our spouses. This is what makes Eve so important. She was not created to provide Adam with a servant or to fulfill a biological role. She was the means by which God would reveal himself to a man who wasn't paying attention.

I imagine Eve was the woman of Adam's dreams. The first time he saw her, he realized that God had created a masterpiece. This flawless woman was the glorious climax of creation. Perhaps Adam understood intuitively, that he and Eve were going to change the world.

How quickly things went south.

When Adam sinned and God asked him what happened, Adam did not hesitate to blame "the woman you gave me."[8] In other words, it's her fault and your fault. It's not my fault.

In rejecting the Giver and his gift, Adam was out of line. But look at what God said next. He said that Adam's enemy would be defeated by her offspring.[9] Not *their* offspring, but *hers.*

"I'm not giving up on you, Adam. But so that you might learn something about partnership, I'm going to set it up so that your deliverance comes through the women you rejected."

In Adam's confused mind, Eve was the cause of all that had gone wrong. "This partnership experiment was a disaster," he might have said. "I'm better off alone." But God wasn't about to give up.

"Adam, you broke it, but I'm going to fix it. And I'm going to fix it in a way that shows you how much I value broken people, even women who have been rejected by their husbands."

And as the Lord foretold, the first woman became the means by which humanity received the greatest Help of all. Which makes Eve a good helper indeed!

Is a wife merely her husband's helpmate?

Tradition teaches that women were created to serve men, but this interpretation is more Athenian than biblical. The opening chapters of Genesis reveal that women are not only equal partners in a divinely ordained plan to bring heaven to earth, but they are also the means by which husbands may encounter the supernatural grace of God.

A man who views his wife as merely a servant is missing out. She is not the Wooster to his Jeeves; she is his partner in combat, his equal in war. When he is knocked down, she can help him up, and vice versa. Just look at how Eve helped Adam!

If we would see our wives as helpers in a biblical sense, then let us adopt a biblical definition of help. Biblical help is the God-sized help that comes to us through flawed people. It is help beyond anything we can manufacture on our own. It is strength to rise when we have fallen and wisdom to speak when we are speechless. It is grace to heal, guide, forgive, lead, and deliver.

When God commissioned us to rule the earth, he knew we would need his help. His aid comes, as often as not, through imperfect people. Even our wives. Even our husbands.

8. Were Women Created to Serve Men?

If you were recruiting a guest speaker for a women's conference, John Chrysostom, the Archbishop of Constantinople, would not be your first choice. Although Chrysostom was raised by a godly mother called Anthusa, he was also trained by a godless Athenian called Libanius, which may account for his mixed views of women.

Chrysostom said women were weak and fickle and inferior to men. Once upon a time, women were equal with men, he said. But then Eve sinned and now women are subject to their husbands.[1]

John Calvin the French Reformer also said that women are here to serve to their husbands. He said the first woman was "a kind of appendage to the man," and was created "to render obedience to him."[2]

John Knox, the 16th-century founder of the Presbyterian Church, agreed. He said, "Woman in her greatest perfection was made to serve and obey man," and the model wife serves her husband as her lord.[3]

Why would otherwise reasonable men say such unreasonable things? Their sexism was inspired by this verse:

For man did not come from woman, but woman from man; neither was man created for woman, but woman for man.
(1 Corinthians 11:8–9)

If women were created to serve men, as some say, a wife's proper relationship to her husband is that of a servant to her master. But that is not what Paul is saying here.

In the Lord woman is not independent of man, nor is man independent of woman. For as woman came from man, so also man is born of woman. (1 Corinthians 11:11–12a)

This verse demolishes the chestnut that women are inferior. If Eve is inferior because "she came from man," then each man is inferior because he is "born of a woman." Chrysostom and Calvin and others who insist that men are superior to women seem to forget that all men are born of women.

Paul is not saying one gender is better than the other or that men are meant to lord it over their wives. So what does he mean when he says the woman was created for man's sake? He is saying the first woman was created for relationship. God made Eve so Adam would have someone to love.

In the beginning, Adam was alone, and it was not good.[4] If he wanted companionship, he could pet a dog or feed a cat, but that was about it. Then God created woman and the world became an infinitely better place.

Eve was not made to be Adam's servant; she was made to be his lover, the object of his affection. "God adorned Eve like a bride, and brought her to Adam," said the rabbis.[5]

This has enormous implications for the way husbands treat their wives as we'll find out when we get to Chapter 15. It should also affect the way we search for a mate.

Finding the right woman

Proverbs says, "He who finds a wife finds a good thing."[6] But what makes a good wife? Is the ideal wife a soul mate or a servant? A partner or a parlor maid? A man may say he's searching for the right woman, but who is the right woman? What is she like? How will he recognize her?

"Easy. The perfect wife is the woman of Proverbs 31."

For many men, the woman described at the end of the book of Proverbs represents the ideal partner. It's not hard to see why. This woman is wise, strong, industrious, entrepreneurial, and—this is the good part—she earns her own money. This capable woman is not just a homemaker; she is a merchant and a property developer. Yet somehow she finds time to make her own clothes and care for the poor. How does she manage her busy life? She starts working before sunrise and doesn't quit until after sundown. Then she spends her evening feeding and caring for her household.

Phew. I'm worn out just thinking about her.

The capable lady of Proverbs 31 is often held up as a role model for young women. "Be like her and you'll make some man very happy." This is a terrible message to give to our daughters.

There are some good reasons why we might not want to compare ourselves with the woman of Proverbs 31. For starters, she is unlike any woman alive and thus presents a picture of womanhood as unrealistic as Barbie. Then there's her marriage which represents the sort of servile arrangement that is at the heart of patriarchal society. While this woman is working hard in the fields, her husband is sitting in the city gate jawing with his mates.[7] Sure, he's an elder, with an important ministry. But let's face it. She's doing the heavy lifting in this relationship.

Aristotle would have loved this marriage. The husband is governing like a king, while his poor wife is working her fingers to the bone raising the kids and running the farm. Can you imagine Adam and Eve living like this? Can you picture Eve toiling from sun-up to sun-down while Adam basked in the sun? She never would have stood for it.

"Adam, I know I'm your helper, but how about giving me a hand?"

"Sorry honey, but I was born to rule. God said."

"But you're not doing anything. You're just talking to yourself."

"It's called praying. Now be a good wife and fix me a fruit sandwich."

If Adam had been like that, Cain might not have been the first murderer.

The wife of Proverbs 31 is an outstanding woman, and any woman who honors the Lord and takes care of her family is a keeper. But it's a foolish man indeed who prefers a servant to a soulmate and who measures his wife by the lofty standards of this passage.

Marriage and ministry

Some men expect their women to support their dreams. "We need to make sacrifices because God called me to ministry/to write a book/to start a business." Yet it does not occur to them that their wives may have dreams of their own. Which brings me to a letter John Wesley wrote to his wife.

Wesley (1703–1791), one of the co-founders of Methodism, married late and married poorly. His marriage to a widow by the name of Molly Vazeille was an unhappy one. Apparently, Molly was jealous of the amount of time her husband spent establishing the Methodist movement. What Molly didn't understand was that Wesley was an important man doing important things for God. Wesley tried to explain this to his wife in a ten-point letter written for her admonition. In this fascinating piece of correspondence, Wesley tells his wife that he loves her, but says there will never be harmony in their home until she learns her proper place:

> Of what importance is your character to mankind, if you were buried just now? Or if you had never lived, what loss would it be to the cause of God?... Be content to be a private, insignificant person, known and loved by God and me. Leave me to be governed by God and my own conscience. Then shall I govern you with gentle sway, and show that I do indeed love you, even as Christ (loves) the Church.[8]

John Wesley was a great man, but it seems he was not a great husband. Telling his wife that she was insignificant and in need of his governance sounds like something an Athenian would say. The irony is that John Wesley supported female preachers. In many respects, he was ahead of his time. Yet it never seems to have occurred to him that his wife had gifts and talents that weren't being expressed, and that this may have been the source of her frustration.

Wesley placed a higher value on his ministry than his marriage, and he did not consider his wife an equal partner. Sadly, their marriage did not last. Wesley accomplished many great things. One can only wonder at how much more he might have done if he and his wife had embraced and shared each other's visions.

Men like Wesley have long tried to put women in their place. But that place is not the servant's quarters; it is on the throne beside them. Wives were not put on this earth to supply their husbands' needs or fuel their ambition. They were created to be their queens, to honor, cherish, and love.

9. Did Jesus Say Infidelity Is the Only Excuse for Divorce? What About Abuse?

Church folk argue much about divorce. Is divorce ever acceptable? If so, when? Some say that divorce is never justified; others say it is under certain conditions.

The Jews of Jesus' day also argued about divorce, and like us, they didn't agree. They fought and bickered and tried to draw Jesus into their debates.

Jesus was a fan of marriage, and he understood that divorce undermines God's plan for partnership. But Jesus never condemned those who had been abandoned or poorly treated by their partners. He spoke up for disenfranchised women such as the *agunahs* or chained wives who had been cast aside by their husbands.

In the Sermon on the Mount, Jesus said this about divorce and remarriage:

> It has been said, "Anyone who divorces his wife must give her a certificate of divorce." But I tell you that anyone who divorces his wife, except for sexual immorality, makes her the victim of adultery, and anyone who marries a divorced woman commits adultery. (Matthew 5:31–32)

The words of Jesus are meant to impart life, but a misreading of this passage brings condemnation and despair. Women have been told, "You cannot leave your violent and abusive husband unless he's been unfaithful." If your husband is intimate with another woman, you can walk away. But if he beats you black and blue, you have to stay there and take it.

Was Jesus saying that infidelity is the only grounds for divorce? Was he deaf to the cries of those suffering domestic violence? Something doesn't add up.

Divorced over dinner

Jesus came to defend women against injustice and abuse. As we saw in Chapter 4, Jewish women suffered in the form of quickie divorces and abandonment. This is the issue Jesus was addressing in the Sermon on the Mount.

"It has been said." What has been said? Jesus is referring to the Law of Moses:

> If a man marries a woman who becomes displeasing to him because he finds something indecent about her, and he writes her a certificate of divorce, gives it to her and sends her from his house... (Deuteronomy 24:1)

What makes a wife indecent or unclean to her husband? Schools of Jewish thought were divided on this issue. The Beit or House of Shammai said uncleanness meant unfaithfulness. It was only lawful to divorce your wife if she had committed adultery. However, Beit Hillel said you could divorce your wife if she did anything displeasing, such as putting too much salt on your dinner.[1]

It seems a frivolous debate to us, but this issue divided the Pharisees. This is why they asked Jesus, "Is it lawful for a man to divorce his wife for any and every reason?"[2] They wanted Jesus to pick a side.

At first, Jesus sidestepped the issue by saying we shouldn't be getting divorced at all. But when pressed to interpret Moses' Law, he came down squarely on the side of Shammai. "Whoever sends away his wife, except for immorality, and marries another woman commits adultery."[3]

In other words, you can't divorce your wife over a burnt or salty meal, but if she has taken another partner, your marriage may be over.

But what if your partner is abusive? What then?

Box 9.1: Domestic abuse in the church

Church leaders sometimes promote a patriarchal picture of a marriage where the men rule gently but firmly while their wives submit meekly and without question. This picture is presented as scriptural, but it can lead to strife and abuse.

A 2018 study done in the UK reported that 42 percent of churchgoers had experienced some form of abusive behavior in their relationships. The women in the study reported emotional abuse (43 percent), physical abuse (27 percent), and sexual abuse (24 percent), and more than half of the perpetrators were Christians. Interestingly, 43 percent of victims said they would not seek support from their churches because they perceived the church lacked expertise in these matters.[4]

A controversial 2017 report published by the Australian Broadcasting Commission claimed that churches were not only failing to address domestic violence, in some cases they were also enabling and concealing it.[5] However, that may be changing as more churches and denominations are taking a public stand against domestic violence.

On ministry websites, it is increasingly common to find position statements defining and condemning different types of domestic abuse. Some ministries even provide practical responses to abuse. For instance, the Salvation Army website mandates that a victim of abuse "should not be further exposed to abuse through misuse of biblical principles, such as, 'wives submit to husbands' or, 'forgive one another.'" It also indicates that the organization stands ready to alert authorities, and to help victims regardless of who the perpetrator is.[6]

Beaten and blamed

Domestic abuse is the silent shame of the church. Research shows that the prevalence of abuse among churchgoers is higher than expected, and that pastors don't talk about it and wouldn't know what to say if they did (see Box 9.1: Domestic abuse in the church). What would Jesus say about domestic abuse? The Lord's heart was to protect the weak and downtrodden. He would have told abuse victims to run, not walk, to safety. There is never any excuse for abuse. Homes ought to be safe places for all.

That is what Jesus would say, but in fact, Jesus said almost nothing at all. Why didn't Jesus talk about domestic abuse? Some say it's because Jewish husbands don't beat their wives like Christian men.[7] As distasteful as that sounds, there is a measure of truth behind it. Although Jewish men have long enjoyed preferential privileges in marriage, their behavior has traditionally been constrained by the law and monitored by religious courts. A Jewish man who beat his wife or failed to provide for her could be compelled to divorce her.[8] In contrast, Christian men can get away with murder.

A young mother called Jane told me she had been assaulted by her husband while pregnant. She was beaten so severely that she lost her baby and nearly died. When she disclosed the assault to church leaders, she was told to stay with her attacker because "God hates divorce." If she left him, they said, "God would never bless you." She was also advised to review her sins and ask her husband for forgiveness.

Stories like this testify to the perverse power of patriarchal religion. Women are not only beaten, they are blamed for the violence they receive. "If your husband struck you, you must've done something to provoke him. Go home and apologize, and try to be a better wife."

Thankfully, Jane did not heed this instruction. She took her surviving daughter and left.

A victim of adultery

Now we come to the second part of the Sermon on the Mount passage. "Anyone who divorces his wife, makes her the victim of adultery." This is an odd thing to say. Some translations say, "Whoever divorces his wife causes her to commit adultery." Again, it doesn't make sense. If your spouse divorces you, how does that make you an adulterer?

Jesus is talking about a problem that was prevalent in Jewish society, namely wife dumping. As we have seen, some men were sending their wives away without giving them divorce certificates. Those same men were then remarrying making their first wives the victims of adultery. Alternatively, the cast off wives were remarrying and unwittingly committing adultery.

Jesus is not condemning these abandoned women; he's defending them from their negligent husbands. He's quoting the Law of Moses because it's the only language these loveless lunkheads understand.

"You wouldn't break the law would you?"

"Definitely not, Jesus."

"And you wouldn't cause someone else to break the law?"

"No sir."

"Yet that's what you are doing when you send your wives out for no reason. You're breaking the seventh commandment."

Jesus was an equal opportunities defender. He used the law to protect women from their lawbreaking husbands, and he also spoke up for men who had been dumped by their unfaithful wives. "If a woman puts away her husband and marries another, she commits adultery."[9]

The short version: stop fooling around and stay faithful to your spouse.

Love in the age of law

Finally we come to the last part of the passage. "Anyone who marries a divorced woman commits adultery."[10] I trust that by now you realize that when the Bible says divorced woman, it does not mean what we think of as a divorced woman. Jesus is talking about an *agunah*, a dumped woman; a wife who has been sent away or put out of the house.[11]

Let's set the scene. The cast-off wife has been sent from the house. Her husband has remarried and moved on. What is she to do?

Since she has been raised in a patriarchal world, the poor woman has no education and few opportunities for employment. She's going to starve. She needs a husband to provide for her. Another man comes along and offers to marry her. Problem solved. However, since she was not properly divorced from her first husband, he becomes an adulterer. He may not be an adulterer in his heart—he's trying to do the right thing. But in the eyes of the law, he has transgressed. What is such a man to do?

"Here's what you have to do," says Jesus. "If you truly love her, go and find her first husband—the one who dumped her—and get him to do what he should've done in the first place. Make the divorce *kosher*. Get that certificate. Then she will be a free woman and you can marry her without committing adultery."

Jesus covers a lot of ground in two verses, and it's easy to come to all sorts of muddled conclusions. But the short version is he was defending women against an ancient injustice. Contrary to our modern beliefs, Jesus was not saying men and women must remain in abusive situations. Nor was he saying those who get divorced, as we understand that word, are committing adultery.

Some of us have been told that there is never any excuse for divorce, but that is not what the Jews believed. The Jews had rules that protected men and women and provided for their release from unhappy marriages (see Box 9.2: Marriage and divorce in Judaism).

To reiterate, Jesus was opposed to divorce. "What God has joined together, let no one separate."[12] But he never condemned the victims

Box 9.2: Marriage and divorce in Judaism

A traditional Jewish marriage has two parts: a betrothal ceremony (*erusin*) followed sometime later, usually a year, by a wedding ceremony (*nisuin*). Documents are signed at each ceremony.

At the betrothal, the promise to marry is formalized with the signing of a *tena'im* or conditions. The *tena'im* is a serious contract that can only be broken by death or divorce.[13] This is why Joseph, who was betrothed but not married to Mary, considered divorcing her after he learned she was pregnant.[14] Joseph could not simply break off the engagement. He had to follow the legal procedure for undoing the betrothal.

At a Jewish wedding, the witnesses sign a *ketubah*. One of the purposes of the *ketubah* is it makes provisions for the wife in the event of divorce. If the couple decides to divorce, they sign a bill of divorcement called a *get*. In Judaism, a husband can divorce his wife, but a wife cannot divorce her husband.[15]

Around the year 1000, Rebbeinu Gershom ben Yehuda (965–1028) decreed that a husband could no longer divorce his wife without her consent.[16] Under Jewish law, a divorced woman may marry just about anyone. However, she cannot marry a priest, and she cannot remarry her former husband if he has remarried in the interim.[17]

of abusive or unfaithful behavior. Nor did he say that such people were adulterers if they remarried.

If you have experienced abuse or infidelity, patriarchal religion will tell you that it's your fault and you can't leave. "Forgive and forget. Make yourself more appealing so he doesn't cheat again. Stop provoking him to violence."

These are not the words of your heavenly Father! God loves you and cares for you. He wants you and your children to be safe and well. Religion will pick up stones to condemn you, but Jesus defends you.

10. Should Women Stay Silent in Church?

Imagine a church where the women are silent. They don't sing, they don't read scriptures, and they don't participate in public prayer. They don't greet their friends or turn to their neighbor and say hello. When the pastor says, "Can I get an 'Amen'?" they don't give him one. Instead, they remain mute. I don't know any church like this, yet this seems to be the ideal according to the Apostle Paul who said, "Women should remain silent in the churches."[1]

I doubt there is a passage in the New Testament that has been mishandled more than this one. What is Paul saying? The Church Fathers took these words at face value. "It is not permitted for a woman to speak in the church," said Tertullian.[2] Many commentators agree. Here is Albert Barnes, the 19th century American theologian:

> Let your women keep silence—this rule is positive, explicit, and universal. There is no ambiguity in the expressions; and there can be no difference of opinion, one would suppose, in regard to their meaning. The sense evidently is, that in all those things which he had specified, the women were to keep silence; they were to take no part.[3]

The Athenians were among the first to say women should stay silent. "Silence is a woman's glory," said Sophocles the playwright.[4] The Greeks liked their women silent, and so did the Jewish rabbis and sages.

But what about Paul? Didn't the apostle say, "You can all prophesy," and "I wish you all spoke in tongues"? Didn't he tell the Corinthians that "when you come together each of you can bring a hymn, a word, a tongue, an interpretation"?[5] How can each of you bring a hymn and a word if half of you must stay silent? How can all prophesy if women must remain silent?

On this question, the scriptures are crystal clear:

Scriptures indicating women can speak in church: Acts 1:14, 2:4,
17, 18, 4:31, 21:9, Romans 12:6, 16:1, 3, 6, 12, 1 Corinthians 12:7,
11, 27, 14:5, 26, 27, 29, 31, 39, 2 Corinthians 5:17, Hebrews 5:12,
1 Peter 2:9, 4:10–11

Scriptures suggesting they can't: 1 Corinthians 14:34

The New Testament is full of exhortations for women to speak
up and participate fully in the corporate life of the church, and no
one banged this drum louder than Paul. So why does he suddenly
change his tune and tell the women of Corinth to remain silent? He
doesn't. Read his words in context and you find he is saying no such
thing. But before we get to the context, let's look at the passage in
question:

> Women should remain silent in the churches. They are not
> allowed to speak, but must be in submission, as the law says. If
> they want to inquire about something, they should ask their own
> husbands at home; for it is disgraceful for a woman to speak in
> the church. (1 Corinthians 14:34–35)

What's going on? Why are Corinthian women told to stay silent
in church and raise any questions to their husbands at home?

According to one interpretation, the uneducated and uncouth
wives of Corinth were interrupting sermons with vocal outbursts.
Being Gentile and unfamiliar with Old Testament stories, they would
shout questions across the aisle to their husbands. However, there
are a couple of problems with this interpretation. While it's true that
male and female Jews sat apart in the synagogues, the Christians did
not, and why would they? And if Gentile wives were unfamiliar with
Jewish stories, why would we expect their Gentile husbands to be
better informed?

Others say that Paul was giving an apostolic commandment.
"Women must remain silent, as the law says." Only there is no law,
at least not in the Bible. Even if there were such a law, don't you find

it strange that the apostle of grace was preaching law? "You are not under law—except the law that says women must remain silent." It makes no sense.

Clarifying context

This is one of those scriptures where the context makes everything clear. The women in the Corinthian church came in two varieties; some were Greek, and some were Jewish. Thanks to Aristotle et al., the Greek women were forbidden by civic law from speaking in public assemblies, and it's *this* law that Paul was referring to.[6] It was the Greek authorities, not him, who said women must remain silent.

But the Corinthian church also had Jewish women in it, so it's possible that Paul was alluding to a Jewish law. He may have been referring to rabbinical teachings that were later codified in the Talmud:

Paul: It is a shame for women to speak in the assembly.[7]
The Talmud: It is a shame for a woman to let her voice be heard among men.[8]

According to the rabbis, the ideal woman was silent and out of sight. In the synagogue, she sat quietly while the men did the talking. Who said women must remain silent? The Jews and the Greeks did. But Paul never said it.

Here's what happened: some people in Corinth decided that church would be vastly improved if the women kept quiet. Just like they did in public assemblies and in the synagogues. After all, women talk a lot. Plus they're ignorant and disruptive. But not everyone thought this was a good idea—the women certainly didn't—so the Corinthians argued among themselves. To settle the matter, they decided to put the question to Paul. What did he think about women in church? Did he permit them to talk?

Corinthian questions

The Corinthians had many faults, but one thing they were good at was asking questions. We know this because of the way Paul responds to their many questions in his letter. "Now concerning the things about which you wrote... now concerning virgins... now concerning things sacrificed to idols... now concerning spiritual gifts... now concerning the collection for the saints...."[9] Much of Paul's first letter to the Corinthians consists of his responses to questions they have raised, and that is the case here.

Paul never said women should stay silent in the churches; the Corinthians did. The passage above is an interpolation. It should be in block quotes because Paul is quoting them. He repeats what they said—that women should not be permitted to speak, as the Greek and Jewish Laws say—before giving his response: "What? Was it from you that the word of God went out? Or did it come to you alone?"[10] In other words, "Are you nuts? By commanding women to be silent do you think you are speaking from the heart of the Father? Do you think that you have heard from God?"

The cockamamie suggestion that half the church should stay silent riled Paul. You can almost hear him shouting his reply. Or you would if English Bibles quoted him properly. Consider how Paul's response appears in different Bibles:[11]

NIV: Or did the word of God originate with you?
AKJV: What? Came the word of God out from you?

Paul explodes with a *What?!* yet some Bibles omit this essential word. This is a travesty. We need to feel the heat of Paul's indignation. He can't believe what he's hearing. The Corinthians have fallen off their collective rocker if they think women should stay silent. Paul's outrage is perfectly expressed in the Source New Testament:

Utter rubbish! Did the Word of God come originally from you! Utter rubbish! Were you the only ones that it reached![12]

Paul was totally opposed to the idea of women staying silent, and he wanted the Corinthians to know it.

> If anyone thinks they are a prophet or otherwise gifted by the Spirit, let them acknowledge that what I am writing to you is the Lord's command. (1 Corinthians 14:37)

In other words, "You're quoting law?! I'll give you law. Listen up, because what I have to say is the Lord's command. And if anyone does not agree with me, they are an ignorant yahoo."[13]

Oh what fun it would have been to be in that church when Paul's letter was read out. Those brainiacs who thought women should remain silent would have been squirming in their seats. The vindicated women would have been shouting for joy! They would not have been silent that day.

"What I am telling you now is the Lord's commandment." Paul felt so strongly about this that he laid down the law: Women should not stay silent. And this wasn't one of those grey areas where he might say, "These are my words, not the Lord's." This was a black and white instruction you could take to the bank. "This is the Lord's command!"

Then to wrap it all up, Paul reminds the Corinthians of what he has already told them:

> Therefore, my brothers *and sisters*, be eager to prophesy, and do not forbid speaking in tongues. But everything should be done in a fitting and orderly way. (1 Corinthians 14:39–40)

The Corinthians preferred their wives to be silent queens. But like the American revivalist Charles Finney, Paul understood that "the church that silences the women is shorn of half its power."[14] Every part of the body of Christ, whether male or female, young or old, is needed. Since no believer is excluded from the priesthood of all believers, all should be encouraged to participate in a way that is edifying to the church.

Should women be forbidden to speak in church, as some have said? Far from it! Paul encouraged women to speak, prophesy, sing, speak in tongues, and do whatever is proper and fitting so that the whole church may be built up.

"God is not a God of confusion," said Paul.[15] It's confusing to tell women they can participate in the life of the church, but they must remain silent, and Paul never does this. Instead, he vigorously defends the right of women to speak.

But does this mean women can teach and preach?

11. Can Women Teach and Preach?

Shortly after Pentecost, Peter and John healed a crippled man and were promptly arrested for stirring up trouble. After the Sanhedrin released them, Peter and John went back to their own people and held a praise party. Then this happened:

> After they prayed, the place where they were meeting was shaken. And they were all filled with the Holy Spirit and spoke the word of God boldly. (Acts 4:31)

It was like a second-Pentecost. The Holy Spirit shook the room and the company of disciples, both male and female, became fearless preachers who spoke the word of God boldly.

Can women teach and preach? They did in the Bible. In Acts 2, both male and female believers began to prophesy. Then in Acts 4, they began to preach. When the Holy Spirit moves in power, who can stay silent? "The lion has roared… who can but prophesy?"[1]

Contrary to what many of us have been taught, women in the early church did not sit on the sidelines; they stood shoulder to shoulder with their brothers prophesying and proclaiming God's word.

> What then shall we say, brothers and sisters? When you come together, each of you has a hymn, or a word of instruction, a revelation, a tongue or an interpretation. Everything must be done so that the church may be built up. (1 Corinthians 14:26)

If *each of you* can have a word of instruction or a revelation, then *each of you* can teach and preach. There is no difference. The only requirement for teaching and preaching is the message should strengthen the church. Your gender has nothing to do with it.

If God has given you a passion for teaching and preaching, then teach and preach. End of discussion. Or it would be except the traditions of men have usurped the instructions of scripture. "For the woman taught the man once," said John Chrysostom "and made him guilty of disobedience, and wrought our ruin."[2]

Men like Chrysostom have essentially rewritten the Bible. They have added words to scripture in a nefarious attempt to silence women. "Each of you can bring a word of instruction, *unless you are a woman*. Each of you can have a revelation, *but women are not allowed to share them*. Each of you can have a tongue or an interpretation, *but women can only share them with other women*."

For 2,000 years women who have felt the call of God have been told to remain silent. They have shunted into convents and nunneries, or they've been sent to far away mission fields. Some have even taken vows of silence. Thanks to our Greek and Jewish heritage, women teachers are still considered progressive, even heretical in parts of the church. The early church had female teachers, but the Church Fathers got rid of them.

Which probably explains why we don't have Church Mothers.

The unbroken chain

Jesus said, "Everyone who is fully trained will be like their teacher."[3] Jesus trained his male and female disciples, so that they would become like him. Then he sent them into the world to train others, so that those others could also be like him.

> Therefore go and make disciples of all nations, baptizing them in the name of the Father and of the Son and of the Holy Spirit, and teaching them to obey everything I have commanded you... (Matthew 28:19–20a)

Those who were discipled by Jesus discipled others, and that pattern continued unbroken for centuries all the way to you. Connect the dots. You heard the good news from someone who heard it from someone who heard it from Jesus.

Can women teach and preach? You better hope they can because it's a dead certainty that in the long line of disciples between you and Jesus, there were female teachers. Remove one of them or tell them to be silent and you might not be here.

Mark Twain once quipped, "What would men be without women? Scarce, sir...mighty scarce." The same could be said for Christians. We'd be mighty scarce if it weren't for women. I need only to reflect on my own life to know this is true. When I was a child, three godly women trained me in the ways of the Lord. When I was a young man, three more women encouraged me to step out in faith. I am who I am today because of the grace of God shown to me by those six women.

If one of the disciples had asked, "Lord, how do we disciple nations?" Jesus would have replied, "Do what I do." Jesus preached to crowds of men and women, and he talked to anyone who listened, regardless of their gender. Unlike the rabbis, he permitted women to follow him and sit at his feet, and he trusted them as reliable witnesses of his resurrection.

Did the disciples follow Christ's example? They must have because the early church was full of women who prophesied and preached and discipled others. Who were these women preachers and teachers? We will meet six of them in this chapter and six more in the next.

Phoebe, the Pauline preacher

If a woman got up to preach, what would you do? Would you storm out, vowing never to return? "I can no longer trust the leadership of this church because they let a woman behind the pulpit. That's unbiblical!" Only it's not unbiblical. Women preached in the New Testament.

When the church in Rome received their letter from the apostle Paul, that letter was delivered, and likely read out, by a woman named Phoebe. This is what Paul had to say about her:

> I commend to you our sister Phoebe, a deacon of the church in Cenchreae. I ask you to receive her in the Lord in a way worthy of his people and to give her any help she may need from you, for she has been the benefactor of many people, including me. (Romans 16:1–2)

Paul introduced Phoebe in a manner similar to the way he introduced Timothy to the Corinthians and Epaphroditus to the Philippians.[4] They were his messengers delivering his messages. What do we know about Phoebe? She was a benefactor of many, which is to say she was a patron, a woman set over others. She was a woman of influence, a leader.[5]

When Phoebe read out Paul's letter, were the Romans shocked? Did they walk out in a huff? Paul doesn't give them the option. He says, "Receive her in the Lord in a manner worthy of the saints." In other words, "Don't dismiss her because of her gender. Welcome her in the name of the Lord."

Paul trusted Phoebe. When she read his letter, she would have had to explain some of its content for her listeners. She probably took questions. Phoebe was a mouthpiece for Paul as much as any modern-day preacher.

The letter to the Romans is considered by some to be the most influential epistle ever written. Every great preacher, from Martin Luther, to John Wesley, George Whitefield, Charles Spurgeon, and Billy Graham, has preached from it. Let us never forget that at the head of this long line of esteemed preachers stands a woman hand-picked by Paul.

Junia, the great apostle

Sitting in the Roman church that day was another prominent female leader. Her name was Junia, and we know about her because Paul greets her by name near the end of his letter. From Paul, we learn four things about Junia: she was in Christ before Paul, she'd spent time in prison with Paul, she was an apostle, and Paul thought she was a *great* apostle.[6]

Some dismiss Junia as a woman of no consequence. "She was merely the wife of Andronicus." Some say she wasn't even a woman. "There weren't any female apostles. Paul must've spelled her name wrong." It seems that some would rather rewrite scripture, than accept that there were female apostles in the Bible.

An apostle is an ambassador or a sent one. Like Paul himself, Junia had been commissioned to preach the gospel. We don't know where she preached or for how long, but we do know that she made an impact. "She is outstanding among the apostles," gushed Paul. When you consider who the other apostles were—Peter, James, John, etc.—that's high praise indeed!

Like those men, Junia had been thrown in jail. This would never have happened to a mere Jewish woman or a Greek one. But Christian women were different. Because of Jesus, women like Junia were standing up and speaking out.

Junia had found her voice. She was a holy troublemaker who spoke truth to power, and Paul thought she was great.

Four lionesses

In addition to Junia and Phoebe, Paul greets four other hard-working women in his letter to the Romans. They were Mary, Tryphena, Tryphosa and Persis.[7] These women were fellow servants of the Lord, ministers of the gospel, and "more spirited than lions."[8]

The New Testament church did not forbid women from preaching and teaching, as some do today. Rather, they commended those

Box 11.1: Was Junia the only female apostle in the Bible?

Evangelical Christians barely recognize any female apostles, but in the Bible, there may have been three or more. In addition to Junia, the outstanding apostle, Mary Magdalene is regarded as "the apostle to the apostles," by Catholics, Orthodox believers, Lutherans, and Presbyterians.[9] We know very little about Mary. The Apostle Paul never mentioned her, and nor did the Church Fathers. Like many Jewish women, she was probably illiterate, and this may explain why she wrote no Gospels or letters.

Much has been written about Mary, most of which can be dismissed as pure fancy. What we can say about her is that she witnessed some of the key events in Christ's life. She remained at the crucifixion when the other men fled, and she was Christ's chosen herald of his resurrection. From the book of Acts, we know she was an active figure in the New Testament church.

Another female apostle was possibly the Samaritan woman Jesus met at the well. Orthodox Christians know her as Photini and regard her as "equal to the apostles."[10] According to Orthodox tradition, Photini was baptized by the apostles on the Day of Pentecost and became a missionary to Carthage. Her ministry was so prolific that it attracted the hostile attention of the Emperor Nero, and she was martyred in AD66.

who taught well and received them as messengers of the gospel. Paul in particular recognized the labor of his female coworkers. He encouraged women to preach and teach, and he publicly praised those who did.

So how do we account for his words to Timothy?

A woman should learn in quietness and full submission. I do not permit a woman to teach or to assume authority over a man; she must be quiet. (1 Timothy 2:11–12)

These words have been used to bind women with unholy bonds. "Women can't talk, and they can't teach." Which just goes to show you the damage that can be inflicted by misreading one scripture and ignoring all the rest:

> Scriptures indicating women can teach: Matthew 28:10, 19–20, Luke 6:40, 8:1–2a, John 4:39, Acts 18:26, Romans 12:7, Romans 16:3–5a, 12, 1 Corinthians 14:26, Colossians 3:16, 2 Timothy 1:5, Hebrews 5:12, 1 Peter 2:9, 3:15, 4:10–11

> Scriptures suggesting they can't: 1 Timothy 2:11–12

Can women teach and preach? To this question the Bible delivers an emphatic and affirmative response. So why does Paul cut against the grain with his words to Timothy? Did he momentarily forget the many women who taught beside him? Or are we reading him wrong? It will help if we unpack his words phrase by phrase.

A woman should learn

In the sexist world of Jewish religion, some believed that women should remain uneducated. "Teach your sons but not your daughters," says the Talmud.[11] To teach women, was to cast your pearls before swine.

In his youth, Paul might have agreed with these sentiments. But then he met Jesus and was set free from his prejudice. Paul changed his tune and began teaching women. When he arrived in Philippi, he only taught women.[12]

Like Jesus, Paul championed a woman's right to education. It was important that Timothy understood this. As the leader of a church, Timothy would have felt pressure to conform to Jewish customs and

Box 11.2: The church and the education of women

The value any society places on women is reflected in the opportunities it provides for their education. The Taliban does not educate girls, and women in Nazi Germany were discouraged from higher learning.[13] In low-income countries, girls receive less education than boys. Consequently, two-thirds of the 750 million illiterate adults in the world are women.[14]

Jesus and the early Christians believed women were worth teaching. However, the Church Fathers and later theologians did not share their enthusiasm. Erasmus of Rotterdam (1466–1536), one of the most acclaimed Christian scholars of the Renaissance, articulated the prevailing attitudes of his era when he said, "Just as a saddle is not suitable for an ox, so learning is unsuitable for women."[15]

It was not until the Protestant Reformation that the church finally began to recognize the value of educating women. In a letter to the mayors of German cities, Martin Luther wrote:

Were there neither soul, heaven, nor hell, it would still be necessary to have schools here below. The world has need of educated men and women, to the end that men may govern the country properly, and women may properly bring up their children, care for their domestics, and direct the affairs of their households.[16]

Luther wasn't about to release women from the kitchen, or let them teach in his church, but he understood that the welfare of all requires the education of all.

Greek habits. "Don't conform to this world," said Paul. "Jesus taught women, and so do we."

When Paul said, "Women should learn," he ignited a fire that is still blazing today (see Box 11.2: The church and the education of women). Yet there are three ways we misread his controversial 1 Timothy 2 passage. First, Paul never says, "Let a woman learn in silence," as some translations have it. He says let a woman learn in quietness or stillness. It's similar to the word he employs earlier in the chapter when he expresses his hope that all believers may enjoy peaceful and quiet lives. Paul is saying a woman who desires to learn should submit quietly to God and his gospel, which is something we all must do. Grace is for the humble and teachable. The proud learn nothing.

Second, Paul does not say that women must learn with all submission *to men*. Terrible damage has been inflicted on the body of Christ by adding two words to scripture and insisting that one half submit to the other.

Third, Paul does not say he is opposed to women teachers (far from it!). When he says, "I do not allow a woman to teach or exercise authority over a man," he adopts an unusual choice of words. Instead of using the normal word for authority (*exousia*), he uses a negative verb (*authenteo*), which can be translated as usurp. It means to dominate or boss around. In a literal sense, it can mean to kill with one's own hands.[17] Paul is painting a picture of violent domination, such as might have been associated with the Ephesian cult of Artemis.

Ephesus was home to Artemis, the Greek mother goddess and her fanatical followers. The female priests who served at the Artemision complex were governed by a high priestess, so domineering female leaders were known in that city.[18] The temptation facing the young church was that in throwing off the shackles of male domination, the pendulum might swing too far in the other direction.

In essence, Paul is echoing what Jesus said to the disciples: "The kings of the Gentiles lord it over them, but you are not to be like that."[19] Just as it is wrong for men to lord it over women, it is wrong for women to lord it over men. A godly teacher does not throw their weight around like a tyrant. Instead, they set an example for others to follow.[20]

N.T. Wright has written a thoughtful essay on this passage:

Paul is saying… that women must have the space and leisure to study and learn in their own way, not in order that they may muscle in and take over the leadership as in the Artemis-cult, but so that men and women alike can develop whatever gifts of learning, teaching and leadership God is giving them.[21]

The traditional take on 1 Timothy 2:11–12 is that women can teach women and children, but they can't teach men. But how can the church be built up if one half refuses to listen to the other half? Paul is not suggesting this at all.

Paul valued women teachers, but he also understood that God's plan for partnership is undermined when one gender tries to control another. Whenever men dominate women (as happened in a patriarchal Jewish context) or women dominate men (as was happening in matriarchal Ephesus), the result is oppression and discord. This is why Paul reminds us to serve one another in the love of Christ. The only remedy for unhealthy hierarchy is to put others first.

So far, so good. But what about this passage?

And the things that you have heard of me among many witnesses, the same commit you to faithful men, who shall be able to teach others also. (2 Timothy 2:2, AKJV)

Was Paul saying Timothy should only train men? Was he saying we shouldn't train women? If so, he was adding to the words of Jesus who said, "Make disciples of all nations." Jesus wants us to train anyone and everyone. If they have breath in their body, tell them the good news.

As you can probably guess, Paul was in complete agreement with the Lord. His desire was for Timothy to train any reliable person, male or female. Although some Bibles specify *men*, the word Paul used is *anthropos,* which means human being. It's a word that is sometimes used to denote people in general.[22] Paul is not saying, "Don't teach women." He's saying, "Train up faithful people who will be able to train others."

Which brings us full circle. We fulfill the Great Commission by discipling people who then disciple others. It makes no difference whether the people we train are black or white, male or female, young or old. Followers of Jesus train anyone who wants to learn so that all of us may grow into the whole measure of the fullness of Christ.

12. Can Women Pastor?

The question of whether women can pastor or oversee or lead churches has been debated for hundreds of years. The traditional conclusion is that women cannot do these things. In the Catholic Church and in some Protestant denominations, the ordination of women is expressly forbidden. "While both men and women are gifted for service in the church, the office of pastor is limited to men as qualified by Scripture," says the Southern Baptist Convention Statement of Faith.[1]

Other denominations, such as the Methodists, the Assemblies of God, and the Salvation Army, do not normally discriminate on the basis of gender. However, even in churches that accept female pastors, few female pastors are actually hired (see Table). The women who do get to lead churches tend to be better educated and paid less than their male counterparts.[2]

Table: Percentage of female senior pastors[3]

USA		UK	
Catholic	3%	Anglican	20%
Evangelical	3%	Baptist	14%
Mainline	20%	Pentecostal	17%
Black protestant	16%	Methodist	40%

Before we find out what the Bible says about women pastors, we need to ask, what is a pastor? A pastor is not a CEO or a general or president or a mini-pope. In the Bible, a pastor is a shepherd. A pastor is someone who tends and guides spiritual sheep.[4]

What does a pastor do? In these busy times, pastors are asked to do a hundred different things. But in scripture, pastors do just three things: they set an example for others to follow, they watch over those in their care, and they teach so that the body of Christ may be strengthened and equipped.[5] Not all teachers are pastors, but all pastors are teachers, in one form or another.

Ask a pastor what he does, and he might say something like this:

My name is Tom. I'm a pastor here. It's my job to pray for you, whether you're a Christian or not, and to talk with you about Jesus, whether you're a Christian or not. That's what I do.[6]

It will help if we distinguish genuine and counterfeit pastors. A true shepherd points to the Good Shepherd who gave his life for his sheep. They fulfill the words of the Lord who said, "I will give you shepherds after my own heart, who will feed you on knowledge and understanding."[7] A good pastor helps you grow in the grace and knowledge of Jesus.

Sadly, some leaders act nothing like shepherds. Instead of serving the body of Christ, they lord it over others in the pursuit of personal gain.[8] Empire builders, rather than kingdom builders, they fail Christ's test for authentic leadership:

You know that the rulers of the Gentiles lord it over them, and their high officials exercise authority over them. Not so with you. Instead, whoever wants to become great among you must be your servant, and whoever wants to be first must be your slave. (Matthew 20:25–27)

A true pastor is a servant, not a lord. They guide rather than control; they feed rather than fleece the sheep. A true shepherd represents the Great Shepherd to the sheep and presents the sheep to the Great Shepherd. Such a person may have a title, such as elder or apostle or pastor, or they may have no title at all. Parents can be pastors. So can school teachers, scout leaders, and soccer coaches. It's not uncommon to find school staff who have pastor in their title or pastoral oversight in their job description. But here we will focus on those who shepherd communities of believers: church pastors. Since an elder or overseer also fits this description, I shall use the terms pastor, elder, and overseer interchangeably.

What do I know about pastoring?

A good writer acknowledges his biases, and it's time I acknowledge mine. I come from a family of pastors. My father was a pastor, my uncle is a pastor, and I have served as a pastor. I have been an active member of pastors' fraternals, and I have ministered in many interdenominational services. I have hosted pastors in my home, and in my travels I have met hundreds of pastors.

I have a soft spot for pastors because I know firsthand the extraordinary challenges they face. I think I know what makes a good pastor, but full disclosure: my views on who can and who cannot pastor have changed over the years.

As a lead pastor of a church in Hong Kong, I taught that women could be deacons but not elders or pastors. Women could lead small groups and teach children, but they couldn't lead the church. I held this position because it was what I had been taught and because that was what the scriptures seemed to say.

I have since learned there is a difference between what the scriptures seem to say and what they actually say. I have repented of my earlier views. It is now my strong conviction that discriminating against women leaders is contrary to God's plan, harmful to the church, and a great loss to the world.

Can women pastor? Let me answer that question with a better one: If God has gifted and called a woman to pastor, should we oppose him? Here's another: Since God empowered women to lead churches in the New Testament, is there any reason to expect that he has stopped doing that today?

Some may say, "No female pastors are named in the Bible." Neither are any male pastors named in the Bible. Search the scriptures and you will find no one identified as Pastor So-and-so.

We live in the age of the celebrity pastor, but the early church had no such thing. What it did have were nameless groups of elders or overseers, such as the Ephesian elders who met with Paul, or the elders Paul greeted at the start of his letter to the Philippians.[9]

That said, the Bible identifies at least three females who pastored, and possibly an additional three. It's time for us to meet these little known ladies.

Pastor Prisca

Prisca was one of Paul's closest friends. They were such dear friends that the apostle called her by the diminutive version of her name, Priscilla. Priscilla and her husband Aquila were Jewish business people who met Paul in Corinth and travelled with him to Ephesus.[10] When Paul left Ephesus, Priscilla and Aquila stayed behind and continued to preach the gospel. Soon they were hosting a church that met in their house.[11] Later, they went to Rome and planted another church. We know this because of the way Paul greets them in his letter to the Romans:

> Greet Priscilla and Aquila, my co-workers in Christ Jesus. They risked their lives for me. Not only I but all the churches of the Gentiles are grateful to them. Greet also the church that meets at their house. (Romans 16:3–5a)

This brief mention speaks volumes. Priscilla and her husband weren't merely homegroup leaders; they were church planters with a multinational legacy. Such was her influence that Paul said the Gentile churches owed Priscilla a debt of gratitude.

What did Priscilla do? To quote Gene Edwards, Priscilla was "Paul's right-hand man."[12] Paul considered her his equal and said she had risked her life for him (like a good shepherd). Priscilla was a pastor to the apostles. She trained Apollos in Ephesus and had two apostles, Andronicus and Junia, in her church at Rome.[13] Priscilla was not merely a pastor; she was a *super*-pastor who raised giants in the faith.

Nympha's church

At a time when the church only met in people's homes, several women were recognized as church leaders. Priscilla was one; Nympha was another. Paul greeted "Nympha and the church that is in her house."[14] We know very little about Nympha. Her house was located either in Laodicea or elsewhere in the Lycus Valley. Was she a pastor? Did she lead the church that met in her house? She must have done so, for Paul greets no one else in her church.

Chloe and her people

Chloe is another one of those intriguing people who is mentioned only once in the Bible. Paul wrote: "I have been informed concerning you, my brethren, by Chloe's people, that there are quarrels among you."[15] We don't know anything about Chloe other than she lived in Corinth and she had people. Who were Chloe's people? Were they her companions or a church that met in her house? We can't be sure. But in the same way that men from James came to Antioch, people from Chloe came to Paul, and he recognized her as a leader within the church community. In short, she was a pastor.

If Paul objected to women pastors, the visit from Chloe's people would have presented him with the perfect opportunity to say so. To quote Tim Fall, Paul could have expressed his concerns like this:

> It has come to my attention you have a woman (Chloe) presiding over a group of brothers and sisters. This must not be! Is there not a man among you who could take over? Don't wait until I am among you to correct this abomination.[16]

Of course, Paul said no such thing, and why would he? Contrary to popular belief, Paul had no problem with women in leadership. Instead of rebuking Chloe's people for putting a woman in charge, he credited them for drawing his attention to a problem. Nice job, Chloe's people.

The Bible seldom names individual church leaders, but we've just met three who were all women. In addition, the scriptures hint at three other women who may have been pastors.

Lydia of Thyatira

Lydia was a Thyatiran trader in purple cloth. When she heard Paul preach the gospel in Philippi, she became a believer, along with her whole household.[17]

Lydia invited Paul and Silas to stay at her home and they agreed. However, on the way to Lydia's house there was a scene involving a demonized fortune teller. Paul cast the spirit out of the girl, and he and Silas ended up in jail. That night an earthquake broke the jail and the following day the two apostles were pardoned by the magistrates. Paul and Silas left town but not without stopping at Lydia's house to encourage the new believers. That's all the Bible has to say about Lydia, but that 24–hour period with Paul was hardly the end of her story.

A generation later, Jesus sent a letter to the church in Lydia's hometown of Thyatira.[18] Who planted this church? Paul never went there. Few people did. Thyatira was an obscure town in the middle of nowhere known for only one thing: purple dye.

Is it possible that the Thyatiran church was planted by the purple cloth dealer from Thyatira who met Paul in Philippi? Did Lydia plant and pastor the church that received a letter from Jesus? It's an intriguing possibility.

The chosen lady of 2 John

The apostle John addressed his second letter to "the lady chosen by God and to her children."[19] Who was this lady and who were her children? Was she a real woman with real children? Or was she a metaphor for the church?

The metaphorical option is weak. The New Testament letters were sent to people. Even when they were sent to churches, someone had to receive the mail and read it. If the dear lady represents the church, who are her children? Also the church? That doesn't make sense. Why would John write a letter "to the church and her church"?

The simplest explanation is the dear lady was the leader of a church, and her children were the people in it. Just as Paul was a mother to the Thessalonians, this lady was a mother to her church.[20] She was a shepherd or pastor.

Interestingly, John never calls her lady or the patronizing "dear lady" of some translations. He calls her *kuria*, which is the feminized version of *kurios*, a word meaning lord or master. She was an important woman, a VIP. Was she a noble woman or a benefactor like Phoebe? Was she Mary, the "chosen" mother of Jesus? We can only guess. But there seems little doubt that she was a pastor of some influence within the church.

The sister of the dear lady

John finishes his letter to the chosen lady with this: "The children of your sister, who is chosen by God, send their greetings."[21] Here is another lady, also called *kuria*, leading a flock of spiritual offspring. We don't know any more about this *kuria* than the first one. But it's reasonable to conclude that both ladies, like Nympha and Chloe, were leaders within the church. Just as Paul acknowledged Priscilla, Nympha and Chloe, these two ladies were pastors, recognized by John.

Can a woman pastor a church? If we are to take the scriptures as our final authority on this question, the answer can only be a resounding yes! In the New Testament, where pastors are generally not named, we have three and possibly as many as six pastors who were clearly women. And these ladies were not renegades operating on the fringes of the church. They were dear friends, co-workers, and pastors to the apostles.

But what about those two scriptures that seem to say women cannot be elders?

The qualifications of an elder

What sort of person makes a good pastor? In his letters to Timothy and Titus, Paul lists sixteen desirable qualities. Pastors or overseers or elders should not be new converts, he says. Nor should they be money-grubbing alcoholics prone to fits of temper. Ideally, they should be good parents because leading a church is like leading a family. And apparently, pastors should also be men:

> This is a true saying: If **a man** desire the office of a bishop, **he** desires a good work. A bishop then must be blameless, the husband of one wife, vigilant, sober, of good behavior, given to hospitality, apt to teach; not given to wine, no striker, not greedy of filthy lucre; but patient, not a brawler, not covetous; one that rules well **his** own house, having **his** children in subjection with all gravity. (For if **a man** know not how to rule **his** own house, how shall **he** take care of the church of God?) Not a novice, lest being lifted up with pride **he** fall into the condemnation of the devil. Moreover **he** must have a good report of them which are without; lest **he** fall into reproach and the snare of the devil. (1 Timothy 3:1–7, AKJV)

In this list, I have underlined ten gender-specific words (man, he, his) that show pastors or elders must be men. This may surprise you, but none of the underlined words are in the Bible. They have all been added by translators. Paul did not say, "If any *man* desire the office of a bishop"; he said, "If any *one*."

Read what Paul actually wrote and you will find his words are remarkably gender-neutral. Which is interesting. If there were ever an occasion to insist or hint that pastors or elders must be men, this was the time. Yet Paul says nothing. Evidently, he did not have a problem with women pastors.

Which begs the question: Why do some English translations insert masculine words where there are none? Either they were translated by people who did not share Paul's views ("A church leader must be a man..." says the New Living Translation. "No he mustn't," said Paul.), or they were translated at a time when *any man* implied *any one*.

We live in an age of heightened gender sensitivity. If the Bible says man, we assume it means man and not men and women. But many of our great Bibles, from the fourteenth century Wycliffe Bible to the King James Version of the early seventeenth century, were translated when such distinctions did not exist. Older Bibles say, "Let your light shine before *men*," while modern Bibles say, "Let your light shine before *people*." Which is better? Either is fine, provided you understand that in older Bibles men implies people. There is no difference. When the angels sang, "Glory to God in the highest, and on earth goodwill toward men," they weren't excluding women from the favor of God.[22] Again, men means people.

Paul never said elders must be men. Not once. The belief that only males can shepherd the church is a malodorous tradition that reeks of Athenian chauvinism.

God made Adam and Eve equal and commissioned them to rule or lead together. However, Paul did include one male-specific word in his list, and that word is husband. To Timothy, Paul said an elder must be the husband of one wife, and he repeated this instruction to Titus:

> For this cause left I you in Crete, that you should set in order the things that are wanting, and ordain elders in every city, as I had appointed you: If any be blameless, the husband of one wife... (Titus 1:5–6a, AKJV)

Since a woman cannot be a husband, she cannot be a pastor or an elder, or so the argument goes. However, this test falls down for two reasons.

First, Timothy, who was in charge of the Ephesian church, did not pass this test. Nor did Paul or Jesus. None of them had a wife. If managing one's household well is a prerequisite for being a shepherd, on what basis could Paul or Timothy oversee any church?

Either Paul was a hypocrite who didn't keep his own rules, or the husband-of-one-wife requirement does not mean what we think it means.

Second, the husband-of-one-wife rule also applied to deacons, yet there were female deacons in the New Testament church.[23] If females can be deacons, they can be elders, and in the Bible, they were.

Paul was a savvy church planter who knew how to recruit pastors. He understood that a shepherd ought to be gentle, peaceable, and all the other things. But why does he have to be a husband of one wife? Because someone who has two or more wives will be a lousy shepherd.

Paul was not ruling out divorced people or celibate people. He was talking about polygamists.

In the world that Paul inhabited, it was not unheard of for a man to have several wives. As we saw in Chapter 4, this happened when Jewish men sent their wives away without issuing certificates of divorce and then remarried. "Such men were adulterers," said Jesus. "And they made bad pastors," added Paul (see Box 12.1: Paul vs the polygamists).

That was Jewish men; Gentile men weren't much better. Among the Romans, marriage was widely regarded as an inconvenience that interfered with a man's natural passions. A wife who cheated could be killed with impunity by her husband, but a man who cheated was untouchable. Consequently, Gentile men were often unfaithful. Even if they were monogamous in marriage, they were polygamous in practice.

A man with multiple wives or mistresses is a faithless man. "Such a man should not be an elder," said Paul. "Instead, recruit reliable people. Choose those who are faithful, not philandering; steady, not shifty; loyal, not lascivious."[24]

Paul never says an elder must be married. He says he must be the husband of *one wife*. It's the number that counts. "If he's married, it had better be to one woman only."

And Paul never says women cannot pastor or shepherd others, for that would contradict everything he believed about the new

Box 12.1: Paul vs the polygamists

Jesus opposed polygamy by rebuking men who remarried without divorcing their wives. Similarly, Paul opposed the practice of polygamy by insisting elders have only one wife. It wasn't just elders. "Each man is to have his own wife, and each woman is to have her own husband."[25]

Like Jesus, Paul challenged the marriage customs of his day. While the rabbis said a man could end a marriage for any number of reasons, such as a failure to produce offspring, Paul encouraged married couples to remain married.[26] Under the Law of Moses, the widow of a man who died was obliged to marry that man's brother.[27] But Paul said a widow was free to marry whomever she wanted, as long as he was a believer.[28]

In the ancient world, polygamy was seen as a solution to the need to provide for women who had lost husbands to warfare and disease. If the church was going to offer a viable alternative to polygamy, it had to solve the problem of what to do with young widows. If you have ever wondered why the New Testament says so much about widows, this is why. To preserve the sanctity of marriage, the church had to provide practical solutions to first-century problems.[29]

creation. Paul was surrounded by women leaders. If he was opposed to women leading, he had ample opportunity to say so. Yet he never did. Instead, he named and praised women leaders repeatedly.

Common objections to women in leadership

Paul endorsed women in ministry, yet many refuse to follow his example. They say things like, "Jesus was a man; therefore, all pastors must be male." By that logic, all pastors should be celibate Jewish carpenters.

"Pastors are shepherds and shepherds are men." Yet there were female shepherds in the Old Testament, and there were several in the new, as we have seen.

"There are no qualification lists in scripture for female pastors." Nor are there lists for *male* pastors. We are not qualified by our gender or marital status; we are qualified by Jesus. Paul told the Ephesian elders they had been qualified to shepherd the church by the Holy Spirit.[30] It is the Lord who calls and equips people to pastor. How can we disqualify those whom God has qualified?

"Women can lead Bible studies in the home, but not in the church building." In the New Testament, there were no church buildings. The church met in people's homes. To lead in the home, as Priscilla, Chloe, Nympha, and others did, was to lead the church. There was no difference.

"Women can preach and teach in the mission field, but not in America." By that logic, it should be acceptable for female missionaries from other countries to preach and teach in America.

"The word pastor is a masculine noun, meant only for men." The word for mankind (*anthropos*) is also a masculine noun, yet it includes everyone. Masculine plural nouns in Greek are often used to describe mixed groups of men and women.[31]

The world needs good shepherds. If God has called you to pastor, don't let anyone stop you. If God is for you, who can be against you?

13. Can Women Lead Men?

The Iranian church is one of the world's fastest growing churches. Since the Revolution of 1979, the church in Iran has grown from a few hundred to nearly a million believers. Much of this rapid growth can be attributed to women leaders working as evangelists and house church leaders. To be a Christian in Iran is to invite imprisonment; to preach the gospel is to risk torture. But nothing stops these courageous women leaders. Like the apostles of old, they preach in public, and when they get arrested, they continue preaching in prison.[1]

Can women lead? It seems a silly question in this day and age, but any church that forbids women from preaching or pastoring or, God forbid, running the show, is saying women cannot lead men. Some object to women in leadership because they believe it is forbidden by scripture. They seem to forget that the Bible is full of stories of women who led.

Then there are those who believe that women are incapable of leading. Aristotle said women were not natural leaders. "The superior male rules, and the inferior female is ruled."[2] Aristotle was a godless Greek but his views on leadership are shared by many Christians. Thomas Aquinas said there would be no order in the human family "if some (meaning women) were not governed by others wiser than themselves (meaning men)."[3]

In other words, women are too dumb to lead. It's an outrageous claim, yet I've had men tell me they have a problem following a woman. They say this because they have been raised in a culture where men rule the roost. The husband makes the decisions, and the pastor is the unquestioned man of God. Because they cannot conceive what it might be like to follow a godly woman leader, they miss out on all that God has for them.

If there were ever an issue where we needed the wisdom of scripture, it's this one. So what does the Bible say about women in leadership?

It will help if we distinguish the verbs rule and lead. None of us is called to lord it over others, but all of us are called to lead, to exercise influence, and to shine. Paul said, "Follow me, as I follow Christ."[4] That's the essence of leadership. We don't follow Paul because he's in charge but because he's going in the right direction. If you are following Jesus, you can lead people who are not. If you are walking in the light, you can guide those who are in the dark.

Can women lead men? They can and they do. They certainly did in the Bible. So far we have looked at a dozen women who led in the New Testament; here are three who led in the Old.

Miriam, the other deliverer

Who led the children of Israel out of Egypt? Most people would say it was Moses, but that answer will only earn you partial credit. The Lord said to Israel, "I sent Moses to lead you, also Aaron and Miriam."[5] The children of Israel were led by three people, one of whom was a woman. Moses was a great leader, but he could not have done what he did without female help (see Box 13.1: The women who made Moses *Moses*).

Was Miriam a good leader? Some dismiss her because of the time she questioned Moses about his foreign wife.[6] Which is a little hypocritical. Moses killed a man, and we forgive him. Hey, we all make mistakes. Let him who is without sin cast the first stone. But Miriam questioned her little brother one time, and she's a Jezebel for life.

We need to give Miriam her proper due. Miriam was a prophetess which meant she spoke for God.[7] Which is kind of a big deal. After the Children of Israel crossed the Red Sea, Miriam led the nation in worship. She wrote a song that made it into the Bible, and her song is still sung today.[8]

These days, it's not uncommon for gifted women to write songs and lead churches in worship, but Miriam was the first. She was the pioneer whose example continues to inspire prophetic worship leaders.

Box 13.1: The women who made Moses *Moses*

Moses is regarded by the Jews as one of the greatest leaders of all time, and rightly so. Moses was a prophet of God and a prince among men. But what few people realize is how there never would have been a Moses except for the intervention of five brave women.

After the Israelites became numerous in Egypt, Pharaoh ordered the slaughter of all Hebrew baby boys. However, two Hebrew midwives, Shiphrah and Puah, refused to obey, and Moses was spared. Pharaoh then ordered the Egyptians to throw the Hebrew boys into the river. This time, baby Moses was protected through the wisdom of his mother, Jochebed, the cleverness of his sister, Miriam, and the mercy of Pharaoh's daughter.

Moses is known as the Deliverer of Israel. But there might never have been a Moses if five women hadn't defied the most powerful man on earth. It was through the courage of these women that God delivered the Deliverer.

Deborah, the mother of a nation

Before Israel was ruled by kings, it was ruled by judges, and the prophet Deborah was one of the best. She was an exceptional leader who led her nation to victory against the technologically superior Canaanites. Why was Deborah a judge? Some say she was the wrong person for the job. God only picked her because there were no good men.

"God's plan is always for men to lead, but when men fail, he will raise up women." Such a claim diminishes both God and women. The Bible is full of stories of God choosing weak men like Moses the murderer, David the adulterer, and Gideon the coward. Male short-comings are no obstacle to God.

Deborah was not God's Plan B; she was God's chosen woman to guide Israel through a time of crisis.

Judge Deborah was a mother to the nation.[9] She would sit under a tree and the sons of Israel would come to her for guidance. On one occasion, Deborah told Barak, the general of Israel's army, to start a war against Sisera the Canaanite commander.[10] Sisera had bullied Israel for 20 years and was a formidable foe. Barak, understandably nervous about leading bronze-aged soldiers against Sisera's iron-wheeled chariots, asked Deborah to go to war with him. Did he need someone to hold his hand? Or did he want Deborah to put her neck on the line as she was asking him to do? Either way, she went, and Sisera and his chariots were routed. By the time Barak caught up to him, Sisera had been killed by a woman with a tent peg.

Deborah was a fearless leader who spoke the word of God to Israel and led from the front. As a result of her leadership, the nation enjoyed peace for forty years.[11]

Huldah, advisor to kings

Like Deborah, Huldah was a prophetess who instructed men in the ways of God. Huldah makes a brief appearance in the history of Israel during the time of King Josiah.[12] The story goes that Hilkiah the high priest discovered the long-lost book of the law. He gave it to Shaphan, the king's secretary, and Shaphan read it to the king. Upon hearing the forgotten law, King Josiah was conscience stricken and tore his robes. He knew Israel was far from God and needed to repent, but how?

Resolving this matter was so important to the king that he formed a taskforce of five eminent men: Hilkiah the high priest, Shaphan the secretary, Ahikam the son of Shaphan, Achbor the son of a prophet, and Asaiah a servant of the king. These men needed a prophet to guide them, and they had access to two of the best: Jeremiah and Zephaniah.[13] However, they ignored these two great men and went to the lesser known Huldah. The prophetess told the king what to do and he submitted to her wisdom.

Why did they choose Huldah over the other prophets? We can only speculate. But their actions were hardly unique. At different times in Israel's history, powerful men looked to women to lead them. Just as Barak went to Deborah, Hilkiah et al. went to Huldah.

If wise women such as Miriam, Deborah and Huldah could lead under the old covenant, they can surely lead under the new, and they did. Women in the New Testament were apostles, prophets, evangelists, pastors and teachers. Many churches today are blessed to have gifted female leaders. William Booth, the co-founder of the Salvation Army, famously said, "Some of my best men are women!"[14]

Yet some refuse to accept the evidence of scripture. They say things like, "Men are uniquely designed to lead." This is simply not true. We are all called to lead, and we can all lead in different ways. There is considerable research showing that female leaders have advantages over their male counterparts.[15] A recent Harvard Business Review study assessing leadership qualities found women outscored men on 17 out of 19 capabilities.[16] A 2019 study from SP Global reported that organizations with female leadership are more profitable and produce superior stock price performance.[17] As Geraldine Ferraro, the first woman to receive a vice presidential nomination from a major American political party, once said, "Some leaders are born women."[18]

I've heard people say, "Men are called to die for their families and churches." Yet throughout history many women have risked their lives for their families and the gospel. Priscilla risked her life for Paul, while Junia the apostle went to prison. Rahab took in the spies of Israel to save her family, while Miriam, Deborah, and Esther put themselves in harm's way to save their nation.

Then there are those who say, "Women are equal; they just can't lead." Which means they are not equal. "Women are equal but they have a different function." That anyone can say this with a straight face is testament to the pervasiveness of gender discrimination. I like Lynn Fowler's response:

How would we react if someone were to say to a black man, "Oh, yes, you are equal to a white man, but you have a different function. Leadership is the function of white men; the function of black men is to be silent and submit"? We would very quickly see that the "equality" being touted by the speaker was most unequal, and in fact a total sham. So why is it that people think they can say to a woman who has the gifts, the training and the calling to lead that this is not her function because she is not male?[19]

Finally, there are those who say women can't lead because the scriptures say that man is the head of woman and women must be subject to men. It is to the subject of headship and submission that we now turn.

14. Should Women Submit to Male Ministers?

A single mother told me about a conversation she had with a church leader:

A church elder told me that he had spiritual authority over me, not in a sexual nature, but in an I-don't-know-what sense. As a newly widowed mother of two young children, I found this man's declaration to be repulsive. Did he say this because I did not have a husband? I doubt that he ever said that to a male congregant.

This elder was hardly alone in saying church men have authority over church women. Many women have heard something similar. "You can preach, but only if there is a male elder present." From where do men get this unholy idea that they're in charge of women? They get it from here:

But I want you to realize that the head of every man is Christ, and the head of the woman is man, and the head of Christ is God. (1 Corinthians 11:3)

This verse, along with 1 Corinthians 11:8–9, which we covered in Chapter 8, is sometimes used to argue that women cannot pastor or oversee or teach men. "Men have a God-given authority over women. Women in the church need to come under the spiritual covering of godly men." However, Paul is not saying this at all. In fact, it is the opposite of what he is saying. Read Paul's entire letter and you will see something like this:

I've heard that you Corinthians are running after certain teachers. Some of you say, "I am of Paul," while others say, "I am of Apollos or Cephas" (1 Cor. 1). This is immature behavior. We are God's fellow workers, so no more boasting about men. All things belong to you and you belong to Christ (1 Cor. 3). Don't put us on pedestals, but regard us as Christ's servants (1 Cor. 4). You've got some issues that I need to address (1 Cor. 5–8), and I'll do that out of my apostolic relationship to you (1 Cor. 9). But the short version is, "follow me as I follow Christ" (1 Cor. 11:1). That's it. Don't put me up like some kind of king. I am not your head; Christ is the head of everyone (1 Cor. 11:3).

Men love to follow men, especially if those men—the ones being followed—are successful or have a good reputation. A man with a gift or a bit of charisma will often find himself surrounded by fans, and this was the case with Paul. His ministry success attracted followers, admirers and acolytes. "Enough of this," said Paul. "We're all servants of Christ."

Who's the head?

Cults form when one person is elevated above others. Paul understood this, which is why he often spoke of the unified body of Christ and being connected to Jesus who is the head of the body.[1] The Apostle Paul is not the head. Nor is the pope or your pastor. Jesus is the head. Submit to him.

He is before all things, and in him all things hold together. And he is the head of the body, the church. (Colossians 1:17–18a)

When it comes to the church, Jesus is the Head with a capital H. There is no part of the church where he is not the head. Nor are there lesser heads. So beware of any leader who says they are your head or spiritual authority.

"But what about delegated authority within the church."

For the sake of order, we need people to lead. Leadership is essential, but a line is crossed whenever obedience is demanded by those "in charge." The do-what-you're-told message is sometimes conveyed subtly via the threat of sticks or the incentive of carrots.

"Disobey God's delegated authority and you are sinning." That's a stick. "Spiritual blessings flow to those under authority." That's a carrot. Neither is scriptural. God's blessings come through Jesus alone.[2]

We don't submit to leaders as though we were soldiers in God's army. We submit out of love and respect because we're family and we recognize the calling of God in their lives. We heed our leaders because they love us and care for us, and people who do that deserve our trust.

A family, not an army

Submission that flows from love releases life, but if you submit to authority out of the fear of punishment or the promise of reward, you have fallen from grace and are no longer walking in love. You have bought into a model of discipleship that has more in common with the pits of Egypt than the New Testament church.

Jesus didn't die to make you a slave, yet some of us have sacrificed our freedom on the altar of patriarchal religion. Instead of practicing the priesthood of all believers, we hire a man to tell us what to do. Jesus is our great high priest, but between him and us we employ a cadre of lesser priests whose word is law. It's as if the old covenant never ended.

How are we to relate to church leaders? The wrong way is to put them on a throne and declare them untouchable. "Never dare to question the Lord's anointed and appointed." But give a man (or woman) that sort of authority, and we are effectively telling the Holy Spirit we don't need him to lead and guide us. "Sorry Jesus, but I belong to Apollos or Cephas. I belong to Pastor Bob." No you don't. You are a free child of God. You belong to no man.

And spare a thought for Pastor Bob. Instead of being surrounded by mature sons and daughters, the poor man is a wet nurse for infantile believers.

Many pastors feel utterly drained from ministering to the sheep. This is because the top-down model of ministry requires constant monitoring and control. It's exhausting. No one can mind the sheep as well as the Good Shepherd. If only there was a better way.

> But God has put the body together, giving greater honor to the parts that lacked it, so that there should be no division in the body, but that its parts should have equal concern for each other. (1 Corinthians 12:24b-25)

There should be no division, says Paul. No clergy/laity distinction and no distinction for gender or race. Each part should have equal concern for one other. Paul is describing a partnership or fellowship where each member is a blessing to the other members. Just as there is no division in a body with some parts more important than others, there should be no division in the church. "Each member belongs to all the others."[3]

It is unbiblical to say some people rank higher than others or that men have spiritual authority over the women. If the great Apostle Paul refused to let others put him on a pedestal, we should be just as reluctant to elevate any man into a position of headship. Let Christ alone be the Head of his church, the only Husband of his bride.

Why does Paul say the man is the head of a woman in 1 Corinthians 11:3? He is not saying one gender is superior to another; he is talking about the marriage relationship. He is saying the husband is the head of the wife. What does that mean? We will find out when we get to Chapter 17. But first we need to look at one of the most misunderstood words in the Bible: submit.

15. Should Wives Submit to Their Husbands?

Lee Grady tells the story of a woman called Doris who suffered through an abusive marriage.[1] Doris's husband, the head deacon at their church, would sometimes come home from work in a rage and physically assault his wife. For a long time, Doris said nothing. But after the violence began to escalate, she turned to their pastor for help. "He's your husband," said the pastor. "You can't leave him. He has authority over you. You must be making him angry."

Doris meekly returned home believing that she was somehow responsible for the abuse she was suffering. Nothing changed. Her husband continued to beat her, and eventually, he killed her.

Doris's story is hardly unique. I have had female readers tell me similar stories. "My husband was abusive, but my church said I had to forgive him and stay with him."

Grady reports that in the United States, religious homes are ranked second highest in incidents of domestic abuse. Only the homes of alcoholics are worse.[2]

Why do so many religious men abuse their wives? It might have something to do with this verse:

Wives, submit yourselves to your own husbands as you do to the Lord. (Ephesians 5:22)

This scripture is part of a two-punch combination that misguided men have inflicted upon women. Apparently, Ephesians 5 says wives must submit to abusive husbands, while Matthew 5 says they can never walk away (see Chapter 9). Of course, these scriptures say no such thing. But read them through a patriarchal lens and you'll think they do.

"Let women be subject to their husbands *as to a lord.*" That's how Thomas Aquinas read Ephesians 5. Aquinas said the relationship between a husband and a wife is "like that of a master to his servant."

Although the husband is not really a lord, his wife submits to him as though he were.[3]

Many Church Fathers and theologians taught that wives are meant to serve their husbands. Augustine said, "It is the natural order among people that women serve their husbands and children their parents, because the justice of this lies in that the lesser serves the greater."[4]

The first duty of a wife, said the Puritan John Dod (1549–1645), is to fear her husband. Her second duty, "is constant obedience and subjection… she must resolve to obey him in all things."[5]

Although the trend these days is towards equality in marriage, much of the Christian world remains committed to traditional roles of hierarchy. And this is understandable, because Paul told wives to submit to their husbands. It's right there in black and white.

Submit. For some, this is the most dangerous word in the Bible. It's medieval. It opens the door to all kinds of abuse. Wouldn't it be better if this explosive word were quietly excised from scripture?

Surely no other word has been the cause of so much physical and psychological damage. But is it possible that submit does not mean what we think it means? Could it be that this word, like the words repent, confess, obedience, and love, has been so mangled by man-made tradition that it no longer bears any resemblance to its original meaning?

What does it mean to submit?

Many years ago, when Camilla and I were writing our wedding vows, my future wife told me that she had a problem promising to submit. We had dug up some traditional vows and one of them riffed on the theme of Ephesians 5. "I promise to love, cherish and submit to my husband as to the Lord."

"I'm not going to say that," said Camilla. I didn't really think she would. Danish women are fiercely independent. They don't submit to anyone anywhere. In the end, we opted for a watered-down version of that passage. But if we were to redo our vows, neither one of us would have a problem saying the word submit. In fact, we would relish it because we have learned the true meaning of submission.

What does it mean to submit?

When we think of submission, we tend to think of the strong dominating the weak. We picture wrestling holds and being beaten into submission. We think of kings ruling over subjects, and husbands lording it over wives. This is the sort of submission that Aristotle wrote about, but it is not what Paul is talking about in Ephesians 5.

Biblical submission stems from love, not power. It is not forced on us from above; it is something we offer to another. It's choosing to surrender because we want to, not because we have to. We yield to the other because we love and respect them. Indeed, submission is the essence of love. It is saying, "Because I love you, I choose to put you first."

Doris did not submit to her husband in love. She submitted because she was told to by powerful men wielding the inviolate commands of scripture. She obeyed because she had been conditioned to believe that God would punish her if she didn't. The awful tragedy is that Doris was killed because of a bad definition of submission.

Telling women or men to submit to abusive partners is like dispensing poison from the pharmacy. It only makes things worse. But coerced submission can also ruin a good marriage. The remedy is not to take a pair of scissors to the submission scriptures; it's the Athenians we need to excise from our Bibles!

Want to know what submission is really like? Look to that harmonious union we recognize as the Godhead. See God the Son submitting in all things to God the Father. See God the Father giving the Son a Name above all names. See the Son bragging about the Spirit, and the Spirit testifying of the Son. There's no ego, no careful guarding of rights, and no anxiety about boundaries. There's just the carefree joy of knowing and being truly known, of loving and being truly loved.

Surely submission is one of God's most beautiful ideas.

Who submits?

In a marriage, who submits to whom? Do husbands submit or wives? Many churchgoers familiar with Ephesians 5 would say that wives submit, but the biblical answer is both. "Submit to one another out of reverence for Christ," said Paul.[6] Husbands put wives first, wives put husbands first, and that's the recipe for a happy marriage (see Box 15.1: The Apostle we read at weddings).

Box 15.1: The Apostle we read at weddings

This weekend, at weddings all over the world, thousands of people will hear the following words from the Apostle Paul: "Love is patient, love is kind, love is not self-seeking."[7] On the subject of love, there was no greater authority. Paul understood that true love does not seek its own, but is other-focused. Love says, "How can I put the needs of the one I love ahead of my own needs? How can I put the other one first?"

The choice to freely give yourself to another human being—a husband, a wife, a child, a friend—for no other reason than *you love them*, is a tremendous risk. It is probably the greatest risk you can take. But when you have someone you truly love, you'll happily take the risk because you love them. And if they happen to love you back—well, there's no greater thrill in the world.

At least that's the theory. In reality, what sometimes happens is that only one of the partners submits, and the result is an imbalanced relationship. Whenever you have a meek wife submitting to a domineering husband or a gentle man yielding to a strong-willed woman, you have a marriage that's out of whack. It will take considerable effort from the long-suffering partner to keep the marriage going.

This is why Paul speaks to both husbands and wives. Like a director dispensing lines in a play, he wants both actors to understand their roles. Husbands are to love their wives as Christ loved his church, and wives are to respect and submit to their husbands, as to the Lord.[8] As long as the husband concerns himself with his part, and the wife concerns herself with hers, all will be well. But as soon as the husband starts reminding the wife of her lines—"Woman, submit!"—there will be trouble.[9]

And trouble there is, because the church teaches only half of Paul's message. It tells wives to submit but it rarely says the same thing to husbands. Which is surprising because in Ephesians, the emphasis is the other way around. Paul spends more time talking to husbands than to wives. Wives get three verses; husbands get nine.[10]

If we are to teach submission, let us do it the way Paul did it. Let us right the imbalances of history by encouraging men to lead the way.

> Wives, submit yourselves to your husbands, as is fitting in the Lord. (Colossians 3:18)

This should not be read as an invitation for the husband to dominate the wife like he's lord of the manor. Instead, it's an invitation for the wife to submit out of love, *as is fitting in the Lord*. In other words, if you want to know what submission is like, look to the One who has a gentle and humble heart. Jesus humbled himself so that we might be lifted up.[11] For similar reasons, a wife puts her husband first to elevate her marriage above the ordinary.

But again, this is only half of the instruction. As in his letter to the Ephesians, Paul has complementary lines for husbands and wives.

"Husbands, love your wives and do not be harsh with them."[12] The word for love (*agapao*) is a verb associated with the unconditional love (*agape*) of God. In other words, if you want to know what real love is like, look to Jesus who laid down his life for you, then do the same for your wife.

Whew! This is some message Paul is preaching. No one ever said anything like this before. In the first century you loved your wife for as long as she provided you with children and didn't over-salt your meals. If she failed to perform, you could trade her for a better model.

"That's not love," Paul would have said. "Loving your wife has nothing to do with her appearance or ability to prepare tasty meals. Nor does it have anything to do with your feelings. True love is intentional. It is choosing to love an imperfect person with the perfect love God has shown you."

It takes two to tango and it takes two loving people to make a good marriage. It's not always easy, but when the husband and wife both respect and prefer one another, the result is a blessed and fruitful partnership.

But who takes the lead?

To someone raised in a culture where the men rule and women do what they're told, a marriage of equals can seem like something out of la-la land. How can a marriage work when there are two chiefs? It works when each chief is totally committed to the success of the other. He plays the supportive husband, and she plays the supportive wife, because both want the best for each other.

Equality in role relationships does not mean both partners take turns doing every household chore. Equality means the husband and wife are equally willing to work hard and make adjustments in their marriage. Decisions are made jointly, and the division of tasks is based on preferences rather than gender stereotypes.

But what if the two chiefs can't agree? What then? When push comes to shove, who gets the final call? Rachel Held Evans offered this answer:

We never really know how to respond to this question because, frankly we don't do a lot of "pushing and shoving" in our relationship. We've never reached the great hypothetical impasse that folks seem so curious about. Even when we disagree, we find compromises based on multiple factors, not a gender-based trump card.[13]

I couldn't agree more. Camilla and I have been married for more than 20 years, and in that time, I can only think of a few occasions when we didn't see eye to eye. Major disagreements just don't come up that often, and when they do, they are usually no match for our mutual love and respect. I'm not saying we're the Von Trapp family singing away our problems, but love conquers all.

Except when it doesn't.

It's a sad fact of life that some marriages break, and people get hurt. Those who promote traditional or patriarchal marriages believe marriages fail when partners are unwilling to accept the roles for which they are designed. "The men don't lead and the women don't submit." If that were true, hierarchical marriages would be the happiest and longest lasting. They are not. Research shows that the divorce rates of Christians are no different from atheists and agnostics.[14]

Marriages fail because the people in them are unhappy, and the unhappiest marriages are the traditional ones. A large study of 50,000 couples found that role relationships have a tremendous impact on marital satisfaction. Most couples in egalitarian marriages (81 percent) are happy, while most couples (82 percent) in traditional marriages are unhappy.[15]

It's no surprise to learn that marriages characterized by mutual respect and equality are happier. What is surprising is that many Christian marriages are intentionally unequal. They are more Athenian than Ephesian, and perhaps this is why our divorce rates are so high. If this upsets you, feel free to direct your anger to Augustine, Aquinas, et al. for selling us a corrupted picture of marriage.

Thankfully, not everyone shares their views about men lording it over wives. Here are some lovely words for husbands that Catholics attribute to John Chrysostom:

Young husbands should say to their wives: I have taken you in my arms, and I love you, and I prefer you to my life itself. For the present life is nothing, and my most ardent dream is to spend it with you in such a way that we may be assured of not being separated in the life reserved for us… I place your love above all things, and nothing would be more bitter or painful to me than to be of a different mind than you.[16]

We have been discussing love and submission, but we have skirted around the issue of who takes the lead in these matters. Jesus does. He leads and guides us and shows us how to love our partners through thick and thin, for richer or poorer, in sickness and in health (see Box 15.2: Marriage advice from Jesus). And Jesus teaches us how to forgive, which is key to success in any relationship.

In a traditional marriage, forgiveness is coerced from the woman. "Forgive his failings because he's your husband." But true forgiveness, like submission, is something we give in response to love. We don't forgive because we're supposed to or because we fear divine wrath. We forgive one other as Christ forgave us.[17]

Your partner will make mistakes, disappoint you, and let you down. When that happens, be quick to forgive. Dispense the patience and compassion that you have received from Jesus. Let his grace heal both your wounds.

Seriously, who's in charge?

Who has the authority in a marriage, the husband or the wife? For much of human history, the men were in charge, and their wives were considered little more than property. Strangely, Paul seems to support this archaic arrangement when he tells the Corinthians, "The wife does not have authority over her own body, but the husband does." In other words, she belongs to him. (Can you see the rabbis and philosophers nodding in agreement?)

Box 15.2: Marriage advice from Jesus

Jesus began his ministry at a wedding. Have you ever wondered what wisdom the Lord might have imparted to the bride and groom as they set out on their marriage journey? He might have said, "You are no longer two, but one flesh." Or he might have reminded them not to be anxious for anything because their heavenly Father cares for them. But I like to think he said something like this: "If you want a great marriage, learn how to serve."

As Jesus said to the disciples, serving others is the path to greatness. "Those who exalt themselves will be humbled, and those who humble themselves will be exalted."[18]

Countless books have been written on how to have a great marriage, but there's no better wisdom than that given by Jesus. If you want to be a great husband or a great wife, make it your habit to serve the other. Learn to excel in serving your partner.

But then Paul follows up with this stunner: "And likewise, the husband does not have authority over his own body, but the wife does."[19] In other words, he belongs to her.

Wait, what? Aristotle would have fallen off his stool. *Men belong to their wives? Has Paul lost his marbles?*

Husbands belong to their wives and wives belong to their husbands, and they both have authority over each other. If this sounds radical, it's because we have forgotten God's original plan. "Two shall become one."[20] When two become one, each partner gives up their right to live independently of the other. Each says, "From now on I belong to you."

For some, this is going too far. "I belong to no one. You'll not tie me to the ol' ball and chain." Some would rather cling to their rights than embrace another person. But marriage is an all-or-nothing proposition. It has to be if the two are to become one. A marriage where only one partner goes all in is like a plane with one wing. She won't fly.

The most quoted woman in the Bible is the Shulammite woman in the Song of Solomon, and she knew a thing or two about love. She was the one who said, "My beloved is mine and I am his."[21] This is the airborne language of love. This woman has been swept off her feet by a man who has fully given himself to her.

A few chapters later she repeats her refrain: "I am my beloved's and my beloved is mine."[22] This woman does not sound like she is chafing under the shackles of wedlock.

Then a third time: "I belong to my beloved, and his desire is for me."[23] Their shared love is so overwhelming, she can't stop talking about it. "We were two, but now we are one, and I couldn't be happier."

When the Shulammite sings, "His desire is for me," it's the same word God used when he said to Eve, "Your desire will be for him." The fall of humanity upset the harmony between the genders, but love rights the scales. "His desire will be for you."

The Shulammite's song is nothing like the shallow songs of the self-absorbed and insecure. Her words testify to the delights of unconditional love and acceptance, and the shared joy of knowing and being known. They tell us that in a relationship between equals, submission is erotic, exciting, sensational!

Want to know what a godly partnership looks like? Then hear the words of the Shulammite. "He desires me, and I desire him. My beloved is mine and I am his."

Equality is not the goal

For much of this book, we have been concerned with equality and restoring women to their rightful place alongside men. If we are to return to God's ways, and follow the example set by Jesus and the apostles, equality and mutual respect are essential. But equality is not the goal; love is. And true love is so other-focused, that equality doesn't come into it.

In a 1943 essay entitled "Equality," C.S. Lewis compared equality to medicine, which is good when we are ill, but is otherwise no good at all. As medicine is no substitute for nourishing food, equality is not the substance of love and life.

> Have as much equality as you please—the more the better—in our marriage laws, but at some level consent to inequality, nay, delight in inequality, (as) an erotic necessity.... Let us wear equality; but let us undress every night.[24]

A good marriage is a partnership between equals who ironically don't see themselves as equal. The husband loves his wife more than his own life, and the wife submits to her husband as to the Lord. Each prefers the other to themselves. In such a marriage, there is no score-keeping to ensure both partners are pulling their weight. Rather, each aspires to love at all times and excel in the gentle grace of giving.

> Be completely humble and gentle; be patient, bearing with one another in love. (Ephesians 4:2)

Now that we have established the biblical meaning of submission, we are ready to answer the question we asked at the start: Should wives submit to their husbands? There are three ways to answer this question. The traditional answer is that wives should always submit because "it's commanded in scripture." However, this approach leads to imbalanced and unhappy marriages that are burdened with the heavy yoke of law. Even if the husband is a good leader and the wife a good follower, the pursuit of intimacy will be frustrated by the partitioning of the partnership. How can they be truly together while he's up there and she's down here?

The egalitarian answer is that wives should never submit because doing so leads to abuse and the perpetuation of patriarchy. However, the egalitarian response, like the traditional one, undermines a marriage for it replaces one law (submission) with another (equality), and any law will minister death. This may come as a shock to those in the egalitarian camp, but the pursuit of equality can shipwreck your marriage. A woman who is mindful of boundaries and maintaining her position may never experience abuse, but nor will she experience authentic love. How can she when her heart is constantly guarded?

The third and best answer to this question is that husbands and wives who freely submit to each other—who are tolerant, tenderhearted, kind and caring, always seeking to edify and serve the other—infuse their marriage with the sweet fragrance of Jesus. In their union, they experience heaven on earth.

Traditional and egalitarian marriages may get a taste, but they never enjoy the full riches of heavenly submission. How can they, when love is demanded rather than given?

A wife who demands respect from her husband denies him the joy of giving it, and in denying him that freedom, she undermines her marriage. But a wife who dares to surrender, who gives respect and trusts her husband, will inspire him to joyfully go all in. Her vulnerability will empower him to love far more than he might have accomplished on his own because this is what we were made for. This was the experience of the Shulammite woman. She risked her heart and went all in. So did her beloved. And as the updraft of their love filled the wings of their relationship, they soared to the highest heights.

That Shulammite woman had it good. But what if you don't? What if your husband doesn't want to submit? What if he acts like he's lord of the manor and king of the castle? In short, what can you do if your husband is a jerk?

16. What If Your Husband Is a Jerk?

Xerxes, the king of Persia, was a bad husband. He treated his wife poorly, slept with other women, and acted like he was king of the castle. Which he was. On one occasion, King Xerxes threw a drunken party for his mates. Thinking he might impress them, he summoned his trophy wife, the lovely Queen Vashti. However, the sensible Vashti refused to come. She had no interest in being ogled by her husband's boozy friends.[1]

Vashti's refusal alarmed the men. "Women should do what they are told. If our wives hear about this, there will be trouble." Fearing Vashti's disobedience would embolden their wives, the men plotted to make an example of her. "Ditch your wife and pick a new one," they told the king. "And this time, get one who does what she's told."

So the king dumped the noble Vashti and went hunting for a replacement wife. Being a superficial man, he decided the best way to do this was to hold a beauty pageant. And by beauty pageant, I mean a spend-the-night-with-the-king contest.

Esther was a young Jewish girl whose family had been taken into captivity. She pleased the king and became his new queen, but she was a queen on a leash. She did not share the king's throne. She could not even enter his presence unless invited. Unlike Vashti, Esther would know her place.

Sometime later, one of the king's men, Haman, introduced a law that threatened the extermination of the Jews. The king foolishly signed the law, and the Jews were doomed. What could Esther do?

If Esther had been a fighter, she would have picked up a sword and led her people in a violent struggle for freedom. But Esther was no Joan of Arc. She was not cut from the same cloth as Jewish liberators such as Deborah. Esther was into cosmetics and perfumes.

When her cousin Mordecai challenged her to confront the king, Esther chickened out. And who can blame her for wanting to keep a low profile? Approaching the king uninvited meant certain death. Even if the king did receive her, what could she possibly say to change his mind? Xerxes was not known as a man who cared for the opinions of his wives.

How to talk to a foolish husband

It's easy for a wife to submit to a husband who loves her like Jesus, who cares for her and lays down his life for her, but what if he's a sexist pig like Xerxes? What if he's a godless heathen who mocks her faith, drinks to excess, and gambles their savings away?

In Chapter 9, we looked at what to do if your husband is abusive, but what do you do if he's just not on the same page? What if he's an unbeliever?

> Wives, in the same way submit yourselves to your own husbands so that, if any of them do not believe the word, they may be won over without words by the behavior of their wives, when they see the purity and reverence of your lives. (1 Peter 3:1–2)

If your man is less than he could be, love him anyway. Love is not a feeling but a choice, and it's a choice made without regard for appearances or behavior. Love is a gift, not a reward.

If your husband is not the man he might be, the temptation may be to write him off or settle for a second-rate marriage. "A better strategy," says Peter, "is to own the situation." Don't wait for your fairy godmother to wave her magic wand and make things better. Step up and take the lead.

Is your husband an unbeliever? Then pray for him. In your actions, reveal Jesus to him. Don't love him more when he goes to church or less when he doesn't. Love him unconditionally as Christ loves you. Unconditional love is winsome. It melts hard hearts and penetrates thick skulls.

A believing wife is a priest in her marriage. Through her loving deeds and gentle speech, says Peter, she may lead her man to Jesus.[2]

"Submit yourselves to your husbands in the same way..." In the same way as what? In the same way that Christ submitted himself to us, even when we treated him badly. Christ loved us while we were sinners. We scorned him yet he did not retaliate. We rejected him, yet he bore the pain of injustice.[3] In the same way, submit to your husband, so that he may be won over. Of course, this should not be read as "let him abuse and beat you." If you are a victim of domestic violence, run, don't walk, to safety. But as God has given grace to you, sow grace and kindness into your marriage.

Of course, there are no guarantees. Your husband may be won over, or he might not be. But you are more likely to reap grace if you sow grace. This principle also applies to men who are married to unbelieving wives. "Husbands, in the same way be considerate with your wives, and treat them with respect."[4] Like Paul, Peter delivered the same message to both husbands and wives. Be respectful. Honor them. Put them first.

> Finally, all of you, be like-minded, be sympathetic, love one another, be compassionate and humble. Do not repay evil with evil or insult with insult. On the contrary, repay evil with blessing, because to this you were called so that you may inherit a blessing. (1 Peter 3:8–9)

Marriages characterized by mutual respect and compassion endure. They weather storms and go the distance because they are grounded in the unfailing love of God. Sadly, not every marriage is like this. Sometimes one partner reads the marriage script, but the other doesn't. Something like this happened to Queen Esther.

What can Esther teach us about submitting to bad husbands?

Esther provides a textbook example of how a wise wife can turn the heart of a foolish husband. When we left Esther, she was the silent queen refusing to approach the king. However, Mordecai convinced her to take the risk, and in she went. What she said next saved her nation. "If it pleases the king, let the king come today to a feast that I have prepared for the king."[5]

Xerxes signed his name to a foolish law, but Esther did not come charging in on her high horse. She did not scold or rebuke her man for his monumental lack of judgment. Instead, she spoke softly, as though anticipating Peter's advice to wives. "If it pleases the king." She invited the king to dinner, and after the meal, he asked her what was on her mind. "What is your petition? I will give you up to half my kingdom."

Remarkably, Esther did not tell him. Instead, she repeated her five wise words—"If it pleases the king..."—before inviting him back for another meal. Why did Esther dither? The usual answer is she was battling fear and anxiety. Maybe we should give Esther a little more credit. Perhaps she sensed the time was not right. She knew that her husband was weary from work. Every day he had to deal with rivals and plotters and conspirators like Haman. He was constantly peppered with petitions and every gift came with a hook. Maybe he was worn out from courtly intrigue.

For whatever reason, Esther decided not to add to his burdens. Instead, she offered her man another night away from the pressures of work. Then on the second night, she repeated the same five words: "If it pleases the king..." and made her request known.[6] Esther dared to speak against the crime committed against her people, and her husband repented of his mistake.

Esther submitted to her husband and through gentle words and respectful behavior, she turned him from his foolish path. Esther was a silent queen no more. She found her voice and thank God she did.

What if Esther had taken a stand?

The Bible records the tale of another foolish king, Nebuchadnezzar of Babylon. This king insisted on threat of death that his subjects worship a large idol. Three Jewish men, Shadrach, Meshach, and Abednego, refused to bow and were summoned to the king to give a "please explain." Their defiant behavior provides an interesting counterpoint to that of gentle Esther.

King Nebuchadnezzar, we do not need to defend ourselves before you in this matter. If we are thrown into the blazing furnace, the God we serve is able to deliver us from it, and he will deliver us from Your Majesty's hand. (Daniel 3:16–17)

While Esther spoke with a submissive attitude of "if it pleases the king," these young men took a more brazen tone. "We don't need to defend ourselves to you." Esther prepared a banquet for her foolish king, but the young men dared theirs to toss them in the furnace, and he did.

In both stories, God worked miraculously, but in different ways. In Esther's story the Lord worked behind the scenes, while in the other, he made a dramatic last-minute appearance to save the day. What do we take from this? Perhaps the Lord did not physically appear in Esther's story because he was already there, revealed in the humble conduct of the Jewish queen. In saving a nation by risking her life, Esther foreshadowed the Deliverer who would die to save the world.

What do we learn from these stories? Make ultimatums like the three young men, and you could end up in the proverbial furnace. But speak gently like Esther, and you may change the heart of a foolish man.

17. Is the Husband the Head of His Wife?

Since time immemorial, men and women have been trying to get along, and the results have been occasionally spectacular but often mixed. Even if you accept that men and women are equal in grace, there are undeniable differences between the genders. What do these differences mean, and how do they affect the way we relate to each other? Do they illuminate that ancient question of *who's the boss?*

Indeed they do, said Aristotle. Since women are excitable, while men are cool, calm and collected, wives need the steady hand of their husbands to guide them. An ideal marriage, said the philosopher, is one where the rational man rules his emotional wife the same way a soul rules its body.[1]

"What nonsense," said the Apostle Paul. "A man is not the soul of a marriage. He's the head."[2] But what does that mean? According to the English theologian Matthew Poole, it means the husband is in charge:

The man is called the head of the woman, because by God's ordinance he is to rule over her. He has an excellency above the woman, and a power over her.[3]

Like Aristotle, Poole believed the husband to be superior to the wife for the same reason that "the head in the natural body, being the seat of reason, and the fountain of sense and motion, is more excellent than the rest of the body."[4]

Albert Barnes, an American theologian, said that the headship of the husband meant the complete subjection of the wife.

In all circumstances—in her demeanor, her dress, her conversation, in public and in the family circle—(she) should recognize her subordination to him.[5]

For 2,000 years, theologians have been parroting Aristotle's dribble about husbands being the rational rulers of their marriages. Wives are delicate creatures, easily upset. They need the cool-headed authority of their superior husbands.

But Jesus said no such thing, and nor did the apostles. When Paul said the husband is the head of the wife, he did not mean he is the king or the boss of the home. He was talking about actual heads, like the one found on the top of your neck. "Husbands ought to love their wives as their own bodies."[6] Just as a head supports the body, the body supports the head. Paul was talking about the unity of marriage and how husbands and wives are mutually dependent.

> For the husband is the head of the wife as Christ is the head of the church, his body, of which he is the Savior. (Ephesians 5:23)

Paul is not saying husbands are their wives' saviors; Christ alone is our Savior. But the manner in which Christ saves—by laying down his body for the church—is the manner in which a husband serves his wife.

> Husbands, love your wives, just as Christ loved the church and gave himself up for her. (Ephesians 5:25)

Just as the love of God is revealed in a death, biblical headship is revealed in sacrifice. In the same way that Christ gave himself up for the church, the husband gives himself up for his wife. He crawls through traffic, fights grizzly bears, and catches bullets for her. He puts her needs and interests ahead of his own because he values her more highly than his own life.

The head is not the boss

Aristotle said husbands rule their wives like kings, and Paul replies, "More like King Jesus." Christ nourishes and cherishes his church. He cares for it and helps it grow.[7] In the same way, a husband cares for his wife as he cares for his own body.

The wrong way to read these headship scriptures is to conclude that the husband is in charge or more in tune with the Lord. "The husband is the priest in the marriage." Nope. The husband and wife are both royal priests, ministering to each other and in team together.

"The husband is head of the home." This is one of those statements that sounds biblical but isn't. It was Aristotle who said, "Every house is under one head," meaning the husband. Paul never said this.

Interestingly, the Bible uses two different words when discussing the head of the home. When Jesus talks about the head of the house knowing the time of the thief's coming, he uses a noun (*oikodespotēs*) which is related to the word despot. A despot is a ruler who holds absolute power. It's the householder or the person in charge of an estate. It's the landowner who hires the vineyard workers or sends his slaves to invite people to a banquet. In context, it means *the man in charge*.[8]

But when Paul talks about husbands being the head of their wives, he uses a different word (*kephalē*) which simply means head. Paul never uses the despot word except when counseling young women "to marry, to have children, and manage their homes."[9] The word for manage (*oikodespoteō*) is the verb form of the word despot. So Paul is instructing the women to be masters or lords of their homes. In the words of John Chrysostom, the "woman is assigned the presidency of the household."[10]

Who is head of the home? According to Paul, it is the wife. She is the lord, master, and president of her household.

Aristotle must be spinning in his grave.

What makes the husband the head?

A husband and wife need each other like a head needs a body. Why did God choose the husband to be head over the woman? (That was a loaded question, by the way. He is not *over* her; she chooses to be *under* him just as he chooses to be *under* her in a mutual desire to elevate the other. If this is news to you, reread your marriage vows.)

Headship reflects origin, not authority. The husband is the head because Eve was taken out of Adam. If Eve had been made first, she would have been the head. Adam's headship reflects the order of creation. When people form a queue, the person at the front is at the head of the line. It doesn't mean they're better than those who came later. It simply means they got there first.

Adam was first in the human race. Without Adam, there would have been no Eve, and without Eve, there would have been no more Adams. Since Adam was first on the dance floor, he takes the lead, and he does that by following the sacrificial example of Christ.[11]

So what? Why does this matter?

It matters because God's original plan was for men and women to rule together, but they will never rule unless one of them takes the lead in laying down their life for the other. That someone is the husband.

How does a husband act like a head?

In the Garden of Eden, God told Adam to avoid the forbidden tree. God didn't tell Eve because she hadn't yet been made. It fell to Adam to convey God's will to Eve, and he failed. It was Adam's job to keep the garden serpent-free, and he failed at that too. Adam was the head who didn't lead, and as a result the partnership failed. If Eve had been made first, these concerns would have been her responsibility. But being made second meant she could not succeed unless Adam succeeded.

> God placed all things under his feet and appointed him to be head over everything for the church, which is his body, the fullness of him who fills everything in every way. (Ephesians 1:22–23)

Jesus is the head of everything, and his headship is exercised through the church and for the church. In the same way, a husband's headship is not exercised upon his marriage, but through his marriage and for the benefit of his marriage. A true king does not rule his queen like an Athenian. Rather, he rules with his queen and for the benefit of his queen, like Jesus.

If Paul believed a husband should rule his wife, he would have used words like master and servant. Like Matthew Poole, he would have said the man was superior and more excellent. But he never said that. Instead, he spoke of mutual submission and preferring one another. He spoke of that divine mystery we know as the one-flesh team:

> For this reason a man will leave his father and mother and be united to his wife, and the two will become one flesh.
> (Ephesians 5:31)

Children obey their parents, but when a marriage is formed, everything changes. The daughter no longer submits to her father, for she has become joined to her husband. Her husband is now her head. Similarly, the husband is no longer beholden to his parents, but he submits to his wife. They have become a one-flesh team ready to take on the world.

Just as wives need to be liberated from patriarchal bondage, husbands need to be liberated from the unholy burden that they alone are responsible for all that happens in the home. You and your spouse are a one-flesh team created to lead together.

Partnership is not always easy, especially when you have the weight of tradition pressuring you to conform to ungodly roles and stereotypes. For the sake of your marriage you must resist that pressure. What God has joined together, let no man separate.

The crown upon his head

Women were never meant to be ruled by men, yet because of the Greeks and the patriarchs and the Fall of Man, here we are. If we are to return to God's original plan, we need a better definition of headship, and Jesus is our definition.

If we men are to be godly husbands, let us take our cue from the One who gave his life for his church. A godly head cares for and nurtures his wife. He respects her as a partner in Christ and acknowledges her God-given talents and gifts. He provides for her and seeks to please her. He encourages and comforts her and helps her to walk in the way that God has set before her. He prays for her and with her. He sets an example for her to follow and points her to Jesus in all things.

The primary way in which a husband serves as a head is by loving his wife as his own body and by giving himself up for her. He leads in the art of love. And so does she. His wife is a queen made in the image of God. Filled with the Spirit, she is just as capable of leading as he is.

As the proverb says, "A wife of noble character is her husband's crown."[12] If her husband is the head, then she is the crown that sits upon it.

18. Are Women More Easily Deceived Than Men?

Here's a great question for your next Bible study class: Why do female witches outnumber male witches twenty to one? Strange question? King James didn't think so. When he wasn't overseeing the production of the Bible that bears his name, James was torturing women he believed were witches. James was so obsessed with magic and witchcraft that he wrote a book about it. In it he explains why most witches are women:

As that sex is frailer than man, it is easier for women to be entrapped in these snares of the devil. This was proved to be true by the serpent's deceiving of Eve at the beginning. The devil has been friendlier with that sex ever since. [1]

When it came to women, King James was a total fruit loop. However, his sexism was hardly unique. Adam blamed Eve for his sin, and men have been blaming women for everything ever since. Tertullian, speaking of women in general, said, "You destroyed God's image, man, and on your account even the Son of God had to die." [2]

In other words, ladies, you killed humanity, and you killed Jesus. Nice one. I hope you're happy.

Blaming and shaming women is an ancient and disgraceful pastime. One of the verses that shamers like to quote is this one:

For Adam was formed first, then Eve. And Adam was not the one deceived; it was the woman who was deceived and became a sinner. (1 Timothy 2:13–14)

This verse has been used to keep women in their place and away from positions of influence. Whenever I say things like, "Women need to be encouraged to speak up in church," or "Women make great leaders," I can be sure someone will quote the scripture above and say something like this:

> Eve was deceived, which shows you that women are innately gullible. It's not their fault they can't be trusted. But it's unwise to allow women to preach and teach as they will lead others into deception. For their own wellbeing, they need the firm hand of a man to guide them.

I wish I were making this up. It's nauseating to hear people demean women in this way. Their arguments are not only unscriptural, they make no sense. They lead to absurd conclusions such as these:

Unlike Eve, Adam was not deceived. He sinned with his eyes wide open. Adam trusted the serpent; therefore, men make better preachers.

Uh-huh.

If Eve was deceived, it was because she was badly trained by the only teacher around. Adam heard God's warning, but he did such a poor job passing it on to his wife, that she was deceived by the serpent's lies. Which goes to show that men make better preachers.

Oookay.

Or how about this nugget. Since women are more easily deceived, we should not let them teach anyone except children. They can't teach men, but it's perfectly fine for these dupes of the devil to run our crèches and children's churches.

Makes perfect sense.

As you can see, a lot of rubbish has been drawn out of the Eve-was-deceived verse.

So what is Paul really saying?

He's saying women need to be taught, just like men need to be taught. Remember, Paul lived in a culture that placed little stock on educating women. In contrast, Paul believed the daughters of Eve should have the same learning opportunities as the sons of Adam. "Let a woman learn."[3]

But I am afraid that just as Eve was deceived by the serpent's cunning, your minds may somehow be led astray from your sincere and pure devotion to Christ. For if someone comes to you and preaches a Jesus other than the Jesus we preached, or if you receive a different spirit from the Spirit you received, or a different gospel from the one you accepted, you put up with it easily enough. (2 Corinthians 11:3–4)

Ignorance can lead to deception. We all need to know what God has said lest we be deceived by another Jesus or a different gospel. Paul is not saying women are inferior to men. He's saying, don't neglect to train women. Adam neglected to teach Eve, and as a result, she fell into deception.

Yet there's even more to this passage. It's likely that Paul was also addressing some Gnostic teachings that had surfaced in Ephesus. Gnosticism was a mish-mash of rambling heresies that have been lost to history. We don't know exactly what was being taught, but given the local culture, it's a fair bet there were some in Corinth who believed that Eve or some Artemis-like mother-goddess had created Adam, or that Eve had been the smart one for pursuing knowledge from the forbidden tree. Paul wrote to set the record straight.

Gnostics: "Eve was created first and was the wiser one."
Paul: "No, Adam was created first; Eve was deceived."

Which begs the question, why did Adam do it? Eve was duped, but he wasn't. He knew there would be consequences to their rebellion, yet he partook anyway.

Why'd you eat the fruit Adam?

The Bible doesn't tell us why Adam followed Eve into sin, so we can only speculate. Some say that wicked Eve pressured her reluctant husband into sinning. "Which goes to show you that women are basically witches and should not be allowed to lead men," King James might have said. I prefer Andrew Wommack's take. He believes Adam followed Eve down the path of death because he loved her and could not bear to be separated from her. In doing this Adam modeled what Jesus would do for all of us.[4]

Beautiful.

There is one more puzzling verse we need to address in 1 Timothy 2. It's the one about women being saved through child bearing.

19. Are Women Saved by Making Babies?

"Men are born to rule, but women fulfill their destiny by leading quiet lives at home and raising children." This is the legacy we have inherited from Church Fathers such as Augustine. The venerable Bishop of Hippo, God bless him, thought that women served no purpose other than to make babies. "I do not see in what sense the woman was made as a helper for the man if not for the sake of bearing children."[1]

Martin Luther likewise taught that the chief purpose of women was to reproduce:

Men have broad and large chests, and small narrow hips, and more understanding than women, who have but small and narrow breasts, and broad hips, to the end they should remain at home, sit still, keep house, and bear and bring up children.[2]

No one said it better than one old-timey radio minister who, when asked why women can't preach and teach, replied, "God made roosters to crow and hens to lay eggs."[3]

Raising children is a noble occupation, but the picture of a man ruling from his castle while his wife raises the kids alone, is contrary to God's plan for partnership. It comes from Athens, not Eden. The scriptures are full of exhortations for men to be proactive and engaged fathers.[4] Men and women are both called to raise children.

So why does Paul single out the ladies with this extraordinary verse about childbearing:

But women will be saved through childbearing—if they continue in faith, love and holiness with propriety. (1 Timothy 2:15)

Since Timothy was the leader of the church at Ephesus, some commentators believe this was a local issue. Ephesians worshipped

Artemis, the goddess of childbirth and midwifery. An Ephesian believer facing a difficult birth might be tempted to fall back on old habits and offer sacrifices to Artemis. "There's no salvation there," said Paul. "Continue in the faith and trust God instead."

Others note that Artemis was a virgin who had taken a vow of chastity. It's possible her followers did the same, and this would make Ephesian mothers feel second-rate, as though they had defiled themselves by making babies. "You haven't," said Paul. "Having babies won't cause you to lose your salvation."

A third interpretation, and the one I like best, is that Paul is talking about Eve. In the previous verse, he mentions that Eve was deceived and became a sinner. But that wasn't the end of her story. She was saved through childbearing, meaning her Offspring undid the damage. So this is talking about the glorious salvation wrought by the Savior Jesus who came from the sinner Eve.

"But the passage above refers to *women* being saved, not a single woman." Actually, the word women is not in the original text. It has been added, which is why it appears in italics in some Bibles. Other translations say, "She will be saved through the child-bearing." Whose child-bearing? In the history of humanity, there is only one child who has saved us, and that child is known as the Seed of Eve.

This is how the Message Bible translates Paul's words:

Woman was deceived first ... On the other hand, her childbearing brought about salvation, reversing Eve.
(1 Timothy 2:14–15a, MSG)

Women are not saved by making babies, but women are saved because Eve had a baby. No baby, no Jesus. Which is a lovely way for Paul to close out what he has been saying. "Adam and Eve did not have a good partnership. Because Adam failed to train his wife, Eve fell into deception, and humanity was lost. But God redeemed their mess by giving us a Savior, born from the couple who fell."

But what about the last part of that passage: "If they continue in faith, love and holiness with sobriety." It sounds as though Paul is preaching conditional salvation. "As long as you maintain self-control, you're saved. But have a bad day and you're out." Paul is not saying this at all. Christian, you are one with the Lord and nothing can separate you from his love.

Paul's frequent exhortations to continue in the faith or continue in the grace of God should not be read as threats to your eternal salvation.[5] He's saying, "Don't be tossed and turned, but keep your eyes on Jesus. Continue trusting him and you won't be seduced into dead works or religious superstition."

Jesus is the Author and Finisher of our faith, and he is good to us. He is worth trusting from start to finish.

20. Are Women Weaker?

Running through the tapestry of human history is a sexist thread that says women are weaker and inferior to men. They are second-born and second-best. This is what the philosophers and rabbis taught, as did the Church Fathers and theologians. John Chrysostom said the women in the Bible were occasionally admirable, "yet did they in no case outstrip the men, but occupied the second rank."[1]

Thomas Aquinas said, "Man is more perfect than woman... (and) naturally superior to the female."[2] John Calvin, the so-called reformer, said:

> Let the woman be satisfied with her state of subjection, and not take it amiss that she is made inferior to the more distinguished sex.[3]

Were there ever more shameful examples of male arrogance? Of course, we would never be so churlish to say such a thing. We know better. Science tells us women are anything but weaker. Women have better immune systems, better genes, and they live longer than men. They experience less stress and lower heart disease, and they are much less likely to start wars. Women perform better academically (when given the chance), companies run by women are more profitable, and countries led by women do better at surviving pandemics.[4]

Are women different? Sure. But weaker? Not a chance.

Yet here's a phrase I've heard from the pulpit: "Women are ill-equipped to preach and lead. Women have more compassion, which makes them vulnerable and prone to deception." Which is a roundabout way of saying that women are inferior to men. Since they are weaker, they should never preach. Which makes perfect sense because God only uses strong people, right?

No, wait.

If God chooses the weak to shame the strong, wouldn't that make women better leaders than men?[5]

Weakness is no barrier to God. He can demonstrate his wisdom and power through anyone. But who says women are weaker? Apparently, Peter did:

> Husbands, in the same way be considerate as you live with your wives, and treat them with respect as the weaker partner and as heirs with you of the gracious gift of life, so that nothing will hinder your prayers. (1 Peter 3:7)

Peter is not saying women are too weak to preach or lead. He's saying careless husbands can render their prayers ineffective. But how do they do that? And what makes a woman the weaker partner?

When God made the first man and woman, both were very good. One wasn't weaker or inferior to the other. But after the Fall, everything changed. Suddenly, men and women were no longer on an equal footing. Because of the curse of sin, the woman found herself at a disadvantage. "He will rule over you." If women are in a weaker position, it is because they have been oppressed by a fallen world that favors men.

When Peter refers to wives as the weaker partner, he is not saying that men can do more push-ups than women or that females are feeble. He's saying women are the victims of an ancient prejudice. And he should know. Every time he went to the Temple, Peter passed through the outer Women's Court on his way to the male-only Court of Israel. Every time he went to the synagogue or every time he saw a woman get stoned for adultery, Peter was reminded that women have not had a fair shake. From the day women were born, their rights were weaker, and their prospects were bleaker.

Taking his lead from Jesus, Peter spoke out against this injustice. He encouraged women to prophesy and speak as though speaking the very words of God. He treated women with respect, and he told husbands to treat their wives as fellow heirs of grace. This was a radical notion for Jewish men. Even today some men have trouble accepting their wives as fellow heirs and equal in the Lord.

"My wife is equal with me? I don't think so. She's a weaker vessel who needs to know her place." If that's what you think, your prayers are going to be hindered, because God opposes proud men.[6]

Pride hinders our prayers because those who think they need nothing from God get nothing from God. This is why religious super-stars are often further from grace than tax collectors and prostitutes.[7] As D.L. Moody once said, "It is to the needy that God opens the wardrobe of heaven and brings out the robe of righteousness."[8]

Like racists, sexist people see others as weaker or inferior. They may not say it aloud, but in their hearts they speak the language of the Pharisee. "Thank God I'm not a foreigner or a woman."

If you are not enjoying the grace of God in your life, it may be because you have lorded it over your wife (or husband) when you should have been treating her (or him) as a fellow heir in grace. Do you look down on your partner or do you submit to them in love? Do you make all the important decisions alone, or do you receive the wisdom that God gives to your other half?

Some men treat their wives poorly because that's how they were raised. They don't know any better. If this is you, what can you do? Peter gives practical instruction:

> Be good husbands to your wives. Honor them, delight in them. As women they lack some of your advantages. But in the new life of God's grace, you're equals. Treat your wives, then, as equals so your prayers don't run aground. Summing up: Be agreeable, be sympathetic, be loving, be compassionate, be humble. (1 Peter 3:7–8, MSG)

It's one thing to be humble before the Lord, but Peter exhorts us to be humble with each other and with people who are different from us. "Clothe yourselves with humility toward one another."[9] Women are not inferior, and neither are foreigners, Catholics, Protestants, Democrats, Republicans, divorced people, old people, young people, and single parents.

If you want more of God's grace to flow in your life, learn to see others as Jesus sees them. The world may dismiss some people as weaker or inferior vessels, but God's grace flows through flawed and broken people.

Even our spouses.

A Word After

"There should be no division in the body. Its parts should have equal concern for each other." – Apostle Paul

For hundreds of years, the church has been parroting pagan philosophy, the effect of which has been to keep half the human race subservient, silent, and sidelined. We have hijacked scripture and lied to ourselves in one of the most effective acts of self-destruction the world has ever seen. Unlike racial discrimination, which pits tribe against tribe, sexual discrimination is a devious piece of devilry that pits men against women. It undermines our marriages, enfeebles the church, and impoverishes society.

In the beginning, God called us to be fruitful and multiply. Yet we have been divided and barren. We have sold our sons on the false religion of Patriarchy, and we have allowed our daughters to be shackled by Prejudice.

Enough is enough. It is time for the children of the Most High to speak out against this ancient evil.

"There should be no division in the body," said the apostle, and so say all who have been baptized into Christ. Indeed, is this not the test of our fellowship, that we esteem those the world deems weak and womanly, while giving greater honor to the parts that lack it? We who have learned to see through the eyes of Christ no longer regard anyone from a fallen point of view.

We've come a long way since men like Aquinas went around teaching that women were defective and misbegotten. In our lifetimes, the mainstream church has begun to confront its sexist heritage, which means we're finally heading in the right direction. But there is still a ways to go. If equality is the goal, we are barely halfway there. But equality is not the finish line; it's merely the start line for the new creation. When the church is standing in unity, with more regard for the gifts of the Spirit than the gender of the person who has them, then we will really live.

Maybe you are already there. Maybe your marriage or your church is characterized by authentic love and abounding life. Wonderful! Let your light shine so that others may find their way out of the darkness of disconnection.

Or maybe you are a million miles from the finish line. Maybe you have been unfairly treated on account of your gender. Your gifts have gone unrecognized, your talents are unused, and your dreams are dead and buried. Don't give up; trust in God.

Look at Eve. Her life was over, but then God spoke and set her on a better path. Think about Deborah sitting under her tree. Then God spoke and she saved a nation. Think about Huldah, living in the shadow of two great prophets. Then God spoke and she helped a king. Think about Mary, Esther, Priscilla and Junia who shone like stars in a world run by men.

My prayer is that you have heard God speaking to you through this book. Write down what you have heard, and believe that his word will come to pass. By the grace of God, and through the partnership, of the Spirit you will be fruitful and multiply.

As someone once said, the world is full of people leading lives of quiet desperation. We all need someone to love, and we all wither in isolation. The universal urge for shared experiences testifies to our desire for *koinonia*-fellowship. We crave connection. Is this not the reason why we share posts, updates, recommendations, books, food, expertise, vacations, cars, boats, homes, and gardens? Yet the one thing we seldom share is our true selves. We don't know how. Or we dare not take the risk.

But Jesus leads the way. By giving his all for us, Jesus declares, "You are worth it no matter the cost." His never-say-die love changes us. It gives us the courage to remove our masks, drop our defenses, and be honest with ourselves and each other. Jesus creates the possibility for genuine intimacy and abundant life.

This is where the church can lead the way. Instead of telling people, "you're in," you're out" or "you're the wrong sort of person," we could be revealing the steadfast love of God. Like Jesus, we can speak for those who have been marginalized, and embrace those who have been rejected. By showing people how deeply their Father loves them, we could be the generation that does away with discrimination once and for all. Wouldn't that be something?

The sun of righteousness is rising, and the long night of patriarchy is coming to an end. The kingdom of heaven is at hand, and it is among us. It is revealed wherever the love of Christ is known. It is seen whenever strong men lay down their lives like Jesus. It is heard whenever confident women are silent no more.

Message from the Author

If you enjoyed reading *The Silent Queen: Why the Church Needs Women to Find Their Voice*, why not pass this book on to a friend or someone who might be blessed by it? And if you want others to hear about the good news in this book, please consider posting a short customer review on Amazon or sharing a few words on social media (#thesilentqueen).

Thank you!

Notes

The roar of the Lord

[1] The eight countries that scored full marks for gender equality were Belgium, Denmark, France, Iceland, Latvia, Luxembourg, Sweden, and Canada. Source: World Bank (2020), "Women, Business and the Law 2020," https://open-knowledge.worldbank.org/bitstream/handle/10986/32639/9781464815324.pdf.

[2] World Economic Forum (Dec. 16, 2019), "Mind the 100 year gap," www.weforum.org/reports/gender-gap-2020-report-100-years-pay-equality.

[3] McKinsey Global Institute (Sept. 1, 2015), "How advancing women's equality can add $12 trillion to global growth," www.mckinsey.com/featured-insights/employment-and-growth/how-advancing-womens-equality-can-add-12-trillion-to-global-growth#.

[4] World Health Organization (2013), "Global and regional estimates of violence against women," 2. www.who.int/reproductivehealth/publications/violence/9789241564625/en/.

[5] Girls Not Brides (2020), "Child marriage around the world," www.girlsnot-brides.org/where-does-it-happen/.

[6] A study by the University of Virginia revealed that women have 73 percent greater odds of being seriously injured in car crashes because safety features are designed for men. Source: Fariss Samarrai (July 10, 2019), "New cars are safer, but women most likely to suffer injury," *UVA Today*, https://news.virginia.edu/content/study-new-cars-are-safer-women-most-likely-suffer-injury.

[7] Stats NZ (Aug. 21, 2019), "Gender pay gap unchanged since 2017," website: https://www.stats.govt.nz/news/gender-pay-gap-unchanged-since-2017.

[8] Or NZD400,000, to quote Ann Brower and Alex James' 2020 study, "Research performance and age explain less than half of the gender pay gap in New Zealand universities," *PLoS ONE*, 15(1): e0226392. https://doi.org/10.1371/-journal.pone.0226392.

[9] Elise Gould, Jessica Schieder, and Kathleen Geier (Oct. 20, 2016), "What is the gender pay gap and is it real?" Economic Policy Institute, website: https://www.epi.org/publication/what-is-the-gender-pay-gap-and-is-it-real/

[10] Family Violence: It's Not OK (2020), "Statistics," www.areyouok.org.nz/family-violence/statistics/.

[11] Barna Group (Mar. 8, 2017), "What Americans think about women in power," https://www.barna.com/research/americans-think-women-power/.

[12] The article reported an increase of clergywomen from 2.3 percent in the 1970s to 20.7 percent in 2017. That's a substantial increase, but clergymen still outnumber women four to one, and the proportion is worse for senior positions. Source: Samuel Smith (Oct. 11, 2018), "Number of clergywomen has exponentially increased over last 2 decades, study says, *Christian Post,* https://www.christian-post.com/news/number-of-clergywomen-has-exponentially-increased-over-last-2-decades-study-says.html.

[13] Barna Group (Aug. 13, 2012), "Christian women today, Part 1 of 4: What women think of faith, leadership and their role in the Church,"

https://www.barna.com/research/christian-women-today-part-1-of-4-what-women-think-of-faith-leadership-and-their-role-in-the-church/.

14 J. Lee Grady (2006), *Ten Lies the Church Tells Women*, Charisma: Lake Mary, FL., 2.

15 Hos. 11:10. See also Job 37:4, Jer. 25:30, Joel 3:16, Amos 1:2.

16 1 Pet. 5:8.

17 Charles Joseph Hefele (1750), "Book 8," *A History of the Councils of the Church: Volumes 1 to 5*, www.ecatholic2000.com/councils/untitled-23.shtml.

18 The Council on Biblical Manhood and Womanhood (1988), "The Danvers Statement," https://cbmw.org/about/danvers-statement.

19 Christians for Biblical Equality, "Mission statement," www.cbeinternational.org/content/cbes-mission#CoreValues.

20 1 Pet. 2:9.

21 "Jesus Christ ... the ruler of the kings of the earth ... did make us kings and priests to his God and Father" (Rev. 1:5–6, Young's Literal Translation).

1. Your royal invitation

1 Gen. 1:28, 2:18.

2 Ps. 133:1, Ecc. 4:9a, 12b, Matt. 18:20.

3 Gen. 1:26.

4 Who is "us" in Genesis 1:26? It's possible that God, having identified himself as the unity of *Elohim*, was alluding to that divine yet mysterious partnership we know as the Trinity.

5 *Koinónia* (G2842), Strong's Concordance, https://biblehub.com/greek/2842.htm.

6 Rom. 5:17.

7 See Gen. 2:24.

8 1 Cor. 12:20–26.

2. The silent queen

1 Chris Marriner, (Feb. 12, 2020), "Job ad calls for manager who has a wife with a 'quiet disposition,'" *NZ Herald,* www.nzherald.co.nz/business/news/article.-cfm?c_id=3&objectid=12307862.

2 Sirach 26:1, 14.

3 Gen. 3:17.

4 See Gen. 3:6.

5 Eve spoke a total of 74 words, which is less than the number spoken by Potiphar's wife (99 words, Gen. 39). Even the nameless girls of Zuph had more to say (77 words, 1 Sam. 9:12–13) than the mother of the human race.

6 The exact proportion of Biblical men to women is impossible to calculate owing to the possible duplication of names in scripture. The eight-percent figure comes from the Wikipedia entry for "Women in the Bible."

7 Lindsay Hardin Freeman in her 2014 book *Bible Women: All Their Words and Why They Matter* published by Forward Movement, records the total number of words spoken by women in the Old and New Testaments as 9,317. Freeman identifies 51 female speakers in the Old Testament and 20 in the New.

8 Josephus, *Antiquities of the Jews*, 17.1.3.

9 Old Testament references for polygyny are as follows: Lamech (Gen. 4:19), Esau (Gen. 26:34, 28:8–9, 36:6), Jacob (Gen. 29:21–30, 32:22), Elkanah (1 Sam. 1:2),

David (2 Sam. 3:2–5), and Solomon (1 Kgs. 11:3). The law regarding polygyny is found in Deu. 21:15.

10   Josephus, *Wars of the Jews*, 1.24.2.
11   Gen. 16:3–4, 19:8, Jud. 19:25–28.
12   See Ex. 21:7, Num. 8:24, 30:3–15, Deu. 21:11–14, 22:28–29.
13   Ex. 20:8–12.

3. Athenian supermen

1   Dwight Garner (Mar. 14, 2014), "Who's more famous than Jesus?" *New York Times Magazine,* www.nytimes.com/2014/03/16/magazine/whos-more-famous-than-jesus.html.
2   The mythological origins of women were recorded in the seventh century BC by the Greek poet Hesiod. Apparently, Zeus ordered the manufacture of a "beautiful evil" from whom would descend "a deadly race and tribe of women who live amongst mortal men to their great trouble." Source: *Theogony*, translated by Hugh G. Evelyn-White (1914), 585–590, www.sacred-texts.com/cla/hesiod/theogony.htm.
3   Quoted in Nicolo Benzi (2016), *Philosophy in Verse: Competition and Early Greek Philosophical Thought*, Thesis, Department of Classics and Ancient History, Durham University, 30, http://etheses.dur.ac.uk/11568/.
4   Hesiod, *Work and Days*, 375, 406.
5   Quoted in J.T. Bristow (1988), *What Paul Really Said About Women,* HarperOne, New York, N.Y., 4.
6   Xenophon, *Symposium*, 2:9.
7   Socrates, *Republic*, 5.
8   Xenophon, *Economics*, 7:24–25.
9   Plato said men had superior souls to women and that lazy men would return as women in *Timaeus* (42a and 90e/91a). In his *Republic* (455d) he said women are like men, but weaker. The extended quote comes from *Timaeus* (42b).
10 Aristotle said females were inferior in *Politics,* 1:1254b, translated by H. Rackham, www.perseus.tufts.edu/hopper/text?doc=Aristot.+Pol.+1.1254b&fromdoc=Perseus%3Atext%3A1999.01.0058.
11 Aristotle (350BC), *Politics*, 1:5, translated by Benjamin Jowett, http://classics.mit.edu/Aristotle/politics.1.one.html.
12 *The birth of a daughter*; Sirach 22:3. *Whoever teaches his daughter*; Mishnah Sotah, 3:4. *Man's wickedness;* Sirach 42:14. *A woman's voice*; Tractate Kiddushin 70a:16. *A man may sell his daughter*; Mishnah Sotah 3.8. *Women's wisdom*; Quoted by Rachel Keren (Mar. 20, 2009), "Torah Study," Jewish Women: A Comprehensive Historical Encyclopedia. *Blessed are you*; Shulchan Arukh, Orach Chayim 46:4.
13 Kaufmann Kohler (1906), "Pharisees," *Jewish Encyclopedia*, www.jewishencyclopedia.com/articles/12087–pharisees.
14 Philo, Special Laws, 3.169.
15 Josephus, *Against Apion*, 2:25.

4. God's gift to women

1   John 2:1–11.
2   Gene Edwards (2005), *The Christian Woman... Set Free.* SeedSowers, Jacksonville, FL., 51.

3   Matt. 11:28.

4   John 6:37.

5   Between the Court of Israel and the Temple was the Court of Priests where the priests offered sacrifices on the altar. Jesus could not have entered this court because he was not a Levite. However, all Jewish men could witness the sacrificial activities from the adjacent Court of Israel, and it was here that Jesus would have engaged with priests and religious leaders. There was no Court of the Women in the original temple; it was only added for the second temple built by Herod. Sometime between Solomon and Herod, religious men decided that the temple designed by God could be greatly improved if women were kept out of it.

6   See Mark 12:41–44.

7   The Sages said a man who talks to women too much brings evil on himself, neglects the study of the Law, and will eventually inherit Gehenna (Source: Pirkei Avot, 1:5). To the Jewish mind, Gehenna was synonymous with hell. See Kaufmann Kohler and Ludwig Blau (1906), "Gehenna," *Jewish Encyclopedia*.

8   Matt. 8:15, 26:7–10, Mark 5:41, Luke 13:13, John 11:5.

9   The story of Jesus healing the crippled woman and the reaction it caused is found in Luke 13:10–17.

10   Luke 4:18.

11   Matt. 5:27–28, Luke 7:37–48, 8:48, John 8:3–11.

12   Deu. 24:1.

13   Mishnah Ketubot 7:5, 6. The rule about divorcing barren wives is found in the Babylonian Talmud, Yebamoth 64a.

14   MyJewishLearning.com, "Confronting the issue of *agunot*, or chained wives," www.myjewishlearning.com/article/contemporary-issues-in-jewish-divorce/.

15   In the Old Testament, a man paid a *mohar* or bride price to the father of his bride (see Gen. 34:12, Ex. 22:16-17). Since the *mohar* became an obstacle to marriage during times of economic hardship, it later became part of the *ketubah* or marriage contract signed during the wedding ceremony. The *ketubah* made marriage easier and divorce harder by specifying the amount a man had to pay his wife if he divorced her. Source: Hayyim Schauss (n.d.), "Ancient Jewish Marriage," MyJewishLearning.com, www.myjewishlearning.com/article/ancient-jewish-marriage/.

16   Luke 16:18.

17   Jewish Virtual Library, "Divorce," www.jewishvirtuallibrary.org/divorce-in-judaism.

18   Jewish Virtual Library, "Marriage," www.jewishvirtuallibrary.org/marriage-in-judaism. Yonah Jeremy Bob (July 4, 2018), "What is Israel's position on Bedouin polygamy?" *The Jerusalem Post*, www.jpost.com/israel-news/what-is-israels-position-on-bedouin-polygamy-561665. David Sedley (Dec. 27, 2016), "In defiance of Israeli law, polygamy sanctioned by top rabbis," *The Times of Israel*, www.timesofisrael.com/in-defiance-of-israeli-law-polygamy-sanctioned-by-top-rabbis/.

19   The womanly parables can be found in Matt. 25:1–13 (the ten virgins), Luke 13:21 (the yeast), Luke 15:8–10 (the lost coin), and Luke 18:1–8 (the persistent widow).

20   Luke 18:5, MSG.

21   Matt. 23:37, Luke 13:34.

22   The rabbi's exact words were: "Let words of Torah burn rather than be transmitted to women." Quoted by Benedict Roth (May 11, 2014), "Women should be able to carry the Torah, too," *The Jewish Chronicle*, www.thejc.com/judaism/features/-women-should-be-able-to-carry-the-torah-too-1.54590.

23   See Luke 10:38–42.

24   Matt. 27:55.

25   Bettisia Gozzadini, an Italian lawyer, is believed to have been the first woman to study at university. She received a degree in law from the University of Bologna in 1237. She later became a teacher and according to legend had to wear a veil to avoid distracting her students. Jone Johnson Lewis, in her 2019 article, "A brief history of women in higher education," lists some of the seminaries that were pioneers of higher education for women in the US. (www.thoughtco.com/history-women-higher-ed-4129738). See also, "The first 10 US colleges to go co-ed," on CollegeStats.org (https://collegestats.org/2013/01/the-first-10-u-s-colleges-to-go-co-ed/) and Elizabeth Dearnley's 2018 article, "The remarkable story of the first women to attend a British university," on iNews.co.uk (https://inews.co.uk/news/-long-reads/university-london-first-british-women-female-students-graduates-507725).

26   Luke 9:23.

27   John 4:39.

28   Matt. 28:10, Luke 24:10.

29   Josephus, *Antiquities of the Jews*, 4.8.15.

30   Acts 1:8.

5. What did the apostles think about women in ministry?

1   Acts 1:14.

2   Acts 4:4, 5:14, 6:7, 8:12.

3   Acts 22:4.

4   John Chrysostom, "Homily 31 on Romans."

5   Gal. 3:26.

6   Matt. 1:18.

7   Luke 24:22–23.

6. What did the Church Fathers think about women?

1   *Irish Times* (Aug. 4, 2018), "Second World War pilot who blazed a trail for women flyers," www.irishtimes.com/life-and-style/people/second-world-war-pilot-who-blazed-a-trail-for-women-flyers-1.3585517.

2   Quoted in Henrietta Heald (2020), *Magnificent Women and their Revolutionary Machines*, Unbound.

3   Helena Schrader (2010), "Women in Military Aviation in World War Two," http://helena-schrader.com/womenaviation.html.

4   John Nichol (2018), *Spitfire: A Very British Love Story,* Simon & Schuster: London, 378.

5   *Washington Post* (May 15, 1984), "Equality as her copilot," https://www.washing-tonpost.com/archive/lifestyle/1984/05/15/equality-as-her-copilot/1ea15406-59b9-41f5-a6b8-ae2171fdb0a1/.

6   Clement, *The Paedagogus*, 2:11.

7   Tertullian, *De Cultu Feminarium* (*The Apparel of Women*), 1:2.

[8] Jerome, *Letter 22: To Eustochium*, 19.

[9] Jerome wrote to a man called Lucinius who, along with his wife, had taken a vow of abstinence. "You have with you one who was once your partner in the flesh but is now your partner in the spirit; once your wife but now your sister; *once a woman but now a man.*" Source: *Letter 71: To Lucinius*, 3.

[10] Jerome, *Letter 107: To Laeta*, 13.

[11] Augustine's comments about the low intelligence of women and how they are good for little more than baby-making come from *De Genesi ad Literam* (*The Literal Meaning of Genesis*) (9.5.9 and 11.42). His comments about women not being made in the image of God come from *On the Trinity* (12.7.10). His warning about women being temptresses like Eve comes from his *Letter to Laetus* (243.10).

[12] Theodore Balsamon, *Commentary on Canon 11*, Synod of Laodicea.

[13] Thomas Aquinas, *Summa Theologiae*, 1.93.4.

[14] Ibid., 1.92.1.

[15] Martin Luther, *Table Talk*, 726.

[16] _____, *Commentary on Genesis*, 2.V.27b.

[17] _____, Commentary on Genesis, 1.V.16.

[18] John Calvin, "Commentary on 1 Corinthians 11."

[19] _____, "Commentary on 1 Timothy 2."

[20] _____, "Commentary on 1 Corinthians 14."

[21] Acts 18:26.

[22] 1 Tim. 2:11.

[23] Rom. 16:1.

[24] Php. 4:2.

[25] Speaking to his young wife, Xenophon said: "We know, dear, what duties have been assigned to each of us by God… To be woman it is more honorable to stay indoors than to abide in the fields, but to the man it is unseemly rather to stay indoors than to attend to the work outside." Source: *Economics*, 7:30-31.

[26] Thomas Aquinas, *Summa Theologiae,* "Supplement," 81.3.

[27] Gary K. Clabaugh (2010), "A history of male attitudes toward educating women," *Educational Horizons*, 88 (3), 164–178, https://files.eric.ed.gov/fulltext/-EJ887227.pdf.

7. Are wives merely helpmates?

[1] Thomas Aquinas, *Summa Theologiae*, 1.92.1. Aquinas said women were created to be helpers to men, said, but the only help they could provide was in having babies. Any other sort of help that a man might need would be better supplied by another male.

[2] Matthew Poole, "Commentary on Genesis 2."

[3] John Calvin, "Commentary on Genesis 2."

[4] See Ps. 40:17, 46:1, 115:11, Deu. 33:26.

[5] Ps. 22:19, 28:7, 33:20, 46:1–2, 86:17, 94:17–19, 118:13–14, Is. 41:10,13–14, 50:9, Matt. 15:25, Heb. 4:16, 13:6.

[6] The word for helper, *ezer*, appears 21 times in scripture. In most occasions, the word is referring to God's help (Gen. 2:18, 20, Ex.18:4; Deu. 33:7, 26, 29; Ps. 20:2, 33:20, 70:5, 89:19, 115:9, 10, 11, 121:1, 2, 124:8; 146:5). On four occasions, it is referring to the inadequacy of man's help (Is. 30:5; Ezek. 12:14; Dan. 11:34, Hos. 13:9).

[7]   Gen. 2:23.
[8]   Gen. 3:12.
[9]   Gen. 3:15.

8. Were women created to serve men?

[1]   John Chrysostom, "Homily 9 on First Timothy."
[2]   John Calvin, "Commentary on 1 Timothy 2."
[3]   John Knox (1558), *The First Blast of the Trumpet Against the Monstrous Regiment of Woman*, 5, http://public-library.uk/ebooks/35/36.pdf.
[4]   Gen. 2:18.
[5]   Genesis Rabbah, 18:1.
[6]   Pro. 18:22.
[7]   Pro. 31:23.
[8]   John Wesley (July 15, 1774), "Letter to his wife," http://wesley.nnu.edu/john-wesley/the-letters-of-john-wesley/wesleys-letters-1774/.

9. Did Jesus say infidelity is the only excuse for divorce?

[1]   Mishnah Gittin 9:10. See also Rabbi Steinsaltz (Mar. 11, 2016), "Gittin 90a-b: Grounds for Divorce," Aleph Society, https://steinsaltz.org/daf/gittin90/.
[2]   Matt. 19:3.
[3]   Matt. 19:9.
[4]   Kristin Aune and Rebecca Barnes (2018), "Church responses to domestic abuse: A case study of Cumbria," Coventry University and University of Leicester, https://restored.contentfiles.net/media/resources/files/churches_web.pdf.
[5]   Julia Baird with Hayley Gleeson (Oct. 22, 2018), "'Submit to your husbands': Women told to endure domestic violence in the name of God," *ABC News*, www.abc.net.au/news/2017–07–18/domestic-violence-church-submit-to-husbands/8652028.
[6]   Salvation Army New Zealand, Fiji, Tonga and Samoa Territory, (Aug., 2005), "Positional statement: Domestic violence," www.salvationarmy.org.nz/research-policy/positional-statements/domestic-violence.
[7]   Jewish Virtual Library, "Marriage," www.jewishvirtuallibrary.org/marriage-in-judaism.
[8]   Jewish Virtual Library, "Divorce," www.jewishvirtuallibrary.org/divorce-in-judaism.
[9]   Mark 10:12.
[10] Matt. 5:32, Mark 10:11, Luke 16:18.
[11] This distinction is perfectly clear in those translations that say, "whoever marries a woman after she's been put away commits adultery" (e.g., ASV, BBE, Darby, LITV, RV, YLT).
[12] Matt. 19:6.
[13] Jewish Virtual Library, "Marriage," www.jewishvirtuallibrary.org/marriage-in-judaism.
[14] Matt. 1:19.
[15] Under Jewish law, only a husband can initiate a divorce. But in practice, a Jewish wife can petition a Jewish court to pressure her husband into divorce (or grant a *get*) when the *ketubah* has been violated. Source: Viva Hammer, "Can a woman

initiate Jewish divorce proceedings?" My Jewish Learning, www.myjewish-learning.com/article/can-a-woman-initiate-jewish-divorce-proceedings/.

16   "Rabbenu Gershom ben Yehuda," Jewish Virtual Library, www.jewishvirtuallibrary.org/rabbenu-gershom-ben-yehuda.

17   Dovid Rosenfeld, "Remarrying One's Divorcee," Aish.com, www.aish.com/atr/Remarrying-Ones-Divorcee.html.

10. Should women stay silent in church?

1   1 Cor. 14:34.

2   Tertullian, *On the Veiling of Virgins,* 9.

3   Albert Barnes (1798–1870), "Commentary on 1 Corinthians 14."

4   Quoted in Aristotle, *Politics,* 1:13.

5   1 Cor. 14:5, 26, 31.

6   If you've ever wondered why Paul began his address at the Areopagus by saying, "Men of Athens" this is why (Acts 17:22). The women of Athens weren't there.

7   1 Cor. 14:35, Aramaic Bible in Plain English.

8   There was no Old Testament law forbidding women to speak in the assemblies or synagogues. However, there was a rabbinical tradition that was eventually codified into law and which survives today in the Talmud: "It is a shame for a woman to let her voice be heard among men." Quoted in Kathryn J. Riss (2003), *Journey's End: Removing "Biblical" Barriers Between Women and Their Destiny,* iUniverse, 249.

The British theologian Adam Clarke (1762–1832) was among the first to connect Paul's words with rabbinical rules. In his commentary on this passage, Clarke says the law that Paul mentions, "was a Jewish ordinance; women were not permitted to teach in the assemblies, or even to ask questions." Clarke interprets Paul's words as reinforcing this Jewish law. Source: "Commentary on 1 Corinthians 14."

9   1 Cor. 7:1, 25, 8:1, 12:1, 16:1.

10   1 Cor. 14:36, World English Bible.

11   1 Cor. 14:36. Translations which omit the exclamatory *What?*: ESV, ISV, NASB, NIV, NKJV, and the NLT. Translations which include it: AKJV, AMP, ASV, BBE, and the KJV.

12   A. Nyland (2007), *The Source New Testament With Extensive Notes On Greek Word Meaning,* Smith and Stirling, Parramatta, N.S.W.

13   My paraphrase of 1 Cor. 14:37–38.

14   Quoted in S.J. Grenz and D. Muir Kjesbo (1995), *Women in the Church: A Biblical Theology of Women in Ministry,* IVP Academic, 46.

15   1 Cor. 14:33.

11. Can women teach and preach?

1   See Amos 3:8.

2   John Chrysostom, "Homily 9 on First Timothy."

3   Luke 6:40.

4   1 Cor. 16:10–11, Phil. 2:29.

5   *Prostatis,* Thayer's Greek Lexicon, https://biblehub.com/thayers/4368.htm.

6   Rom. 16:7.

7   Rom. 16:6, 12.

8   John Chrysostom, "Homily 31 on Romans."

9   Pope John Paul II called Mary "the apostle to the apostles" in his letter "Mulieris Dignitatem," Vatican (Aug. 15, 1988), https://w2.vatican.va/content/john-paul-ii/en/apost_letters/1988/documents/hf_jp-ii_apl_15081988_mulieris-dignitatem.html. The Orthodox Church in America recognizes Mary as the "equal of the apostles." Source: "Myrrhbearer and Equal of the Apostles Mary Magdalene," www.oca.org/saints/lives/2016/07/22/102070-myrrhbearer-and-equal-of-the-apostles-mary-magdalene. The Evangelical Lutheran Church in America celebrates an annual feast day for Mary Magdalene and identifies her as an apostle in its booklet, "What is a lesser festival? When and how do we celebrate them?" https://download.elca.org/ELCA%20Resource%20Repository/-What_is_a_lesser_festival_When_and_how_do_we_celebrate_them.pdf. In an article for the Presbyterian Church of Aoteaora New Zealand, Glynn Cardy notes that Jesus commissioned Mary Magdalene "as an apostle to the apostles." Source: "Mary Magdalene: 'Apostle to the Apostles'," The Community of Saint Luke: Presbyterian Church of Aoteaora New Zealand, www.stlukes.org.nz/sermon/mary-magdalene-'apostle-apostles'.

10 Photini is described as "equal to the apostles" in "St. Photini, the Samaritan Woman," Antiochian Orthodox Christian Archdiocese of North America, http://ww1.antiochian.org/st-photini-samaritan-woman, and "The Samaritan Woman: St. Photini," Coptic Orthodox Diocese of the Southern United States, https://suscopts.org/resources/literature/563/the-samaritan-woman-st-photini/.

11 Sifrei Devarim, 46:46.

12 Acts 16:13.

13 Adolf Hitler claimed that women were "equal but different from men," by which he meant that women were inferior. Hitler ruled that women were ineligible for jury service since they were governed by emotion and unable to think logically or reason objectively. Hitler believed in the "natural order" where a woman's life revolves around the three "Ks" of *Kinder, Küche,* and *Kirche* (Children, Kitchen, and Church). In a 1934 speech to the National Socialist Women's League, Hitler argued that for the ideal woman "her world is her husband, her family, her children, and her home."

14 Global Partnership for Education (Sept. 24, 2018), "12 years to break down the barriers to girls' education," www.globalpartnership.org/news/infographic/12–years-break-down-barriers-girls-education.

15 *Colloquia,* quoted in Lesley Ann Greyvenstein (1989), "The development of women for management positions in education," Doctoral thesis, Potchefstroomse Universiteff vir Christelike Hoer Onderwys, 29.

16 Quoted in Lars P. Qualben (1940/2008), *The Lutheran Church in America,* Wipf and Stock, 218.

17 *Authenteo,* Thayer's Greek Lexicon, https://biblehub.com/thayers/831.htm.

18 Acts 19:28. Little is known about the cult of Artemis, but there is evidence that priestly functions in the Artemision were performed by virgin female priests and eunuchs. Source: Jan Bremmer (2008), "Priestly personnel of the Ephesian Artemision: Anatolian, Persian, Greek, and Roman Aspects," The Center for Hellenic Studies, Harvard University.

19 Luke 22:25-26.

20 1 Pet. 5:3.

21 N.T. Wright (2004), "Women's service in the Church: The Biblical basis," http://ntwrightpage.com/2016/07/12/womens-service-in-the-church-the-biblical-basis/.

22 For example, Matt. 5:13, 16, Mark 11:2, 1 Tim. 6:16.

12. Can women pastor?

1 Southern Baptist Convention, "Baptist faith & message 2000," https://bfm.sbc.net/bfm2000/.

2 Barna Group (2009), "Number of female senior pastors in Protestant churches doubles in past decade," www.barna.com/research/number-of-female-senior-pastors-in-protestant-churches-doubles-in-past-decade/#.Vc5b2lNVikp

3 US data come from the 2012 National Congregations Study Wave 3 Report, https://sites.duke.edu/ncsweb/files/2019/02/NCSIII_report_final.pdf. UK data come from Peter Brierley's *UK Church Statistics 2005-2015*, the results of which are summarized in "Statistics on women in ministry" by the Evangelical Alliance (July 2, 2012), https://www.eauk.org/church/research-and-statistics/women-in-ministry.cfm.

4 The word "pastors" appears only once in the Bible, in Ephesians 4:11. However, the Greek noun (*poimēn* G4166), appears eighteen times and in every other case it is translated as shepherd. The terms pastor and shepherd are synonymous. A pastor is someone who shepherds a flock.

5 See Acts 20:28, Eph. 4:11, Tit. 1:9, Heb. 13:17, 1 Pet. 5:2–3.

6 Marshall Shelley (2001), "So what exactly does a pastor do?" *Christianity Today*, www.christianitytoday.com/pastors/2001/march-online-only/cln10314.html.

7 Jer. 3:15.

8 1 Pet. 5:2–3.

9 Acts 20:17, Php. 1:1. Only two elders are named as such in the Bible. (Peter and John identify themselves as elders in their letters.) Paul names many men and women as co-workers, but he rarely specifies their roles or titles. It's as if their titles don't matter.

10 See Acts 18.

11 1 Cor. 16:19.

12 Edwards, *The Christian Woman*, 73.

13 Acts 18:26, Rom. 16:7.

14 Col. 4:15.

15 1 Cor. 1:11.

16 Tim Fall (Jan. 30, 2017), "When a godly woman leads God's people," https://timfall.com/2017/01/30/godly-woman-leads-gods-people/.

17 Acts 16:14–15.

18 Rev. 2:18–29.

19 2 John 1:1.

20 1 Thess. 2:7.

21 2 John 1:13.

22 Luke 2:14.

23 1 Tim. 3:12, Rom. 16:1.

24 In one of the oldest commentaries on this passage, John Chrysostom said Paul was not saying an overseer must have a wife; he was prohibiting his having more than

one. "For even the Jews were allowed to contract second marriages, and even to have two wives at one time." Source: "Homily 10 on First Timothy."

25 1 Cor. 7:2.

26 1 Cor. 7:10–11.

27 Deu. 25:5-6.

28 1 Cor. 7:39.

29 Instructions for taking care of widows can be found in Acts 6:1–4 and 1 Tim. 5:5-16.

30 Acts 20:28.

31 Ephesians 4:11 lists five types of minister: apostles, prophets, evangelists, pastors and teachers. Since the nouns in this list are all masculine, some say that only men can occupy these offices. Yet the Bible identifies female apostles, female prophets, female evangelists, and female teachers. Since the Bible also names at least three women who shepherded churches, there is no scriptural reason to exclude the possibility of female pastors.

13. Can women lead men?

1 Emily Judd (Feb. 11, 2020), "Meet the two women who spread Christianity to hundreds in Iran's Evin prison," *Al Arabiya English*, https://english.alarabiya.net/-en/features/2020/02/11/Meet-the-two-women-who-spread-Christianity-to-hundreds-in-Iran-s-Evin-prison. World Watch Monitor (Jan. 20, 2017), "Women 'central' to spread of Christianity in Iran," www.worldwatchmonitor.org/2017/01/-women-central-to-spread-of-christianity-in-iran/.

2 Aristotle, *Politics*, 1:5. Translated by Benjamin Jowett, http://classics.mit.edu/Aristotle/politics.1.one.html.

3 Thomas Aquinas, *Summa Theologiae*, 1.92.1.

4 See 1 Cor. 11:1.

5 Mic. 6:4.

6 Num. 12:1–9.

7 Jews revere Miriam as one of seven great female prophets. The other six are Sarah, Deborah, Hannah, Abigail, Huldah, and Esther. Source: Megillah 14a.

8 Ex. 15:21.

9 Jdg. 5:7.

10 Jdg. 4:5–7.

11 Jdg. 5:31.

12 2 Chron. 34:14–22.

13 Tamar Kadari (n.d.), "Huldah, the Prophet: Midrash and Aggadah," Jewish Women's Archive, https://jwa.org/encyclopedia/article/huldah-prophet-midrash-and-aggadah.

14 Quoted by Lauren Martin (n.d.), "Some of my best men are women!" *Others Magazine*, https://others.org.au/army-archives/some-of-my-best-men-are-women/.

15 Kenneth Nowack summarizes the evidence in his 2009 article, "Women are better leaders than men. Period," *Envisia Learning*, http://blog.envisialearning.com/women-are-better-leaders-than-men-period/.

16 Jack Zenger and Joseph Folkman (June 25, 2019), "Women score higher than men in most leadership skills," *Harvard Business Review*, https://hbr.org/2019/06/-research-women-score-higher-than-men-in-most-leadership-skills.

[17] Daniel J. Sandberg (Oct. 16, 2019), "When women lead, firms win," *S&P Global*, www.spglobal.com/_division_assets/images/special-editorial/iif-2019/whenwomenlead_.pdf.

[18] Geraldine A. Ferraro (1991), "The future of women in politics," *Archives of Women's Political Communications*, https://awpc.cattcenter.iastate.edu/-2017/03/09/the-future-of-women-in-politics-feb-20-1991/.

[19] Lynn Fowler, (n.d.), "Women," Word and Fire Ministries, https://wordandfireministries.com/women-in-ministry/.

14. Should women submit to male ministers?

[1] Eph. 1:22–23.
[2] Eph. 1:3.
[3] Rom. 12:5.

15. Should wives submit to their husbands?

[1] J. Lee Grady, *Ten Lies….*, 182.
[2] Ibid., 9.
[3] Thomas Aquinas, "Commentary on Ephesians 5."
[4] Augustine, *Questions on the Heptateuch*, 1.153, quoted in "Equality for Catholic women?" http://equalityforwomeninthecatholicchurch.com/?page_id=165.
[5] John Dod, "The duties of husband and wife," *A Puritan's Mind*, www.apuritansmind.com/the-christian-walk/the-christian-family/the-duties-of-husband-and-wife-by-dr-john-dod/.
[6] Eph. 5:21.
[7] 1 Cor. 13:4–5.
[8] Eph. 5:22, 25, 33.
[9] If younger women need training on how to be wives, who should train them? Not their husbands, said Paul, but other, more experienced women (see Tit. 2:3–5).
[10] Paul speaks to wives in Eph. 5:22–24, and husbands in Eph. 5:25-33.
[11] Matt. 11:29, Php. 2:8.
[12] Col. 3:19.
[13] Rachel Held Evans (June 04, 2012), "4 common misconceptions about egalitarianism, " https://rachelheldevans.com/blog/4–common-misconceptions-egalitarianism.
[14] In 1999, the Barna Research Group published the results of a survey of 4000 US adults. They found that 27 percent of Christians had been divorced in comparison with 24 percent of non-Christians. This study created no small stir because it also found that divorce rates were higher (34 percent) for nondenominational protestant churches (read, evangelical Christians) than atheists and agnostics (21 percent). The 1999 study is no longer hosted on the Barna website having been replaced by a more recent one done in 2008. In the newer study, Barna reported that there was no difference between Christians and non-Christians in their divorce rates. Source: Barna Research (Mar. 31, 2008), "New marriage and divorce statistics released," www.barna.com/research/new-marriage-and-divorce-statistics-released/.
[15] David H. Olson, Amy Olson-Sigg, and Peter J. Larson (2008), *National Survey of Married Couples*, Life Innovations, Roseville, MN, www.prepare-enrich.com/-pe/pdf/research/2011/national_survey_married.pdf.

[16] Catechism of the Catholic Church, #2365, www.vatican.va/archive/ccc_css/-archive/catechism/p3s2c2a6.htm.

[17] See Eph. 4:32, Col. 3:13.

[18] Matt. 20:26, 23:12.

[19] 1 Cor. 7:4 (New King James Version). The NIV Bible adds a word which beautifully captures Paul's meaning: "The wife does not have authority over her own body but *yields* it to her husband. In the same way, the husband does not have authority over his own body but *yields* it to his wife."

[20] God's plan, originally quoted in Genesis 2:24, was repeated by both Jesus (Matt. 19:5, Mark 10:8) and Paul (1 Cor. 6:16, Eph. 5:31).

[21] Song of Solomon, 2:16.

[22] Ibid., 6:3.

[23] Ibid., 7:10.

[24] C.S. Lewis (Aug. 27, 1943), "Equality," *The Spectator*, Vol. CLXXI, 192.

16. What if your husband is a jerk?

[1] The story of Xerxes and his two wives is recorded in the Book of Esther.

[2] Paul says something similar in 1 Cor. 7:13–14.

[3] 1 Pet. 2:19–23.

[4] 1 Pet. 3:7.

[5] The story of Esther's invitation to dinner is found in Esther 5.

[6] Est. 7:3.

17. Is the husband the head of his wife?

[1] Aristotle, *Politics*, 1:5, 7. Translated by Benjamin Jowett, http://classics.mit.edu/-Aristotle/politics.1.one.html.

[2] 1 Cor. 11:3, Eph. 5:23.

[3] Matthew Poole, "Commentary on 1 Corinthians 11."

[4] _____, "Commentary on Ephesians 5."

[5] Albert Barnes, "Commentary on 1 Corinthians 11."

[6] Eph. 5:28.

[7] Eph. 5:25-30.

[8] *Oikodespotēs* (G3617). See Matt. 10:25; 13:27; 13:52; 20:1; 20:11; 21:33; 24:43, Mark 14:14, Luke 12:39; 13:25; 14:21; 22:11.

[9] 1 Tim. 5:14.

[10] John Chrysostom, Sermon: "The kind of women who ought to be taken as wives," https://christianhistoryinstitute.org/magazine/article/women-archives-wifes-domain/.

[11] In 1 Corinthians 11:3, Paul says, "Christ is the head of every man." Jesus is not the head because everyone worships and obeys him. (Some don't.) He is the head because he was with God in the beginning and through him all things were made (John 1:2–3). Similarly, the husband is not the head because his wife worships and obeys him. He is the head because Eve came out of Adam.

[12] Pro. 12:4a.

18. Are women more easily deceived?

[1] James Rx (1597), *Daemonologie: In Forme of a Dialogie*, 5:44.

[2] Tertullian, *De Cultu*, 1:2.

3   1 Tim. 2:11.
4   Andrew Wommack, "Commentary on 1 Timothy 2:15," *Online Bible Commentary*, www.awmi.net/reading/online-bible-commentary/.

19. Are women saved by making babies?

1   Augustine, *De Genesi ad Literam (The Literal Meaning of Genesis)*, 2.5.9.
2   Martin Luther, *Table Talk*, quoted in George Seldes (2011), *The Great Thoughts, Revised and Updated: From Abelard to Zola, from Ancient Greece to Contemporary America, the Ideas That Have Shaped the History of the World*, Random House.
3   Letha Dawson (2008), "Nothing new under the sun," *Christian Feminism Today,* https://eewc.com/nothing-new-sun.
4   For example: Deu. 6:6-7, Pro. 4:1–4, 22:6, Luke 15:11–32, Eph. 6:4, Col. 3:21, 1 Thes. 2:11, 1 Tim. 5:8.
5   "Jesus is the source of *eternal* salvation" (Heb. 5:9). For a list of every scripture guaranteeing the believer's eternal security, see my web page, "Eternal Security," https://escapetoreality.org/resources/eternal-security/.

20. Are women weaker?

1   John Chrysostom, "Homily XIII (Ephesians 4:17–19)," www.ccel.org/ccel/schaff/npnf113.iii.iv.xiv.html.
2   Thomas Aquinas, "Commentary on 1 Corinthians 11."
3   John Calvin, "Commentary on 1 Corinthians 11."
4   The Deep Knowledge Group ranks countries for their handling of Covid-19. At the time of writing, three of the world's four safest countries (Germany, New Zealand, and Switzerland) were run by women leaders (Angela Merkel, Jacinda Ardern, and Simonetta Sommaruga respectively). Source: COVID-19 Regional Safety Assessment 250 Countries, Regions & Territories https://www.dkv.global/covid-safety-assessment-250-list (retrieved Sept., 16, 2020). See also Amanda Taub (May 15, 2020), "Why are women-led nations doing better with Covid-19?" *New York Times*, https://www.nytimes.com/2020/05/15/world/coronavirus-women-leaders.html
5   So said Domenica Narducci da Paradiso (1473–1533), a renowned preacher from Florence. In 1500 Narducci was tried for being a scandalous woman who preached illicitly and did not have a regular confessor. Her defense came from 1 Cor. 1:27: "God chose the weak things of the world (i.e., women) to shame the strong." Source: Adriana Valerio (2012), "Narducci da Paradiso Domenica (1473–1533)," *Handbook of Women Biblical Interpreters*, Merion Ann Taylor (editor), Grand Rapids: Baker Academic, 383–386.
6   1 Pet. 5:5.
7   Matt. 21:31b.
8   D.L. Moody (~1891), Sermon: "Saved by Grace Alone," https://biblehub.com/-library/moody/sovereign_grace/chapter_ii_saved_by_grace.htm.
9   1 Pet. 5:5.

Scripture Index

Acknowledgements

I sent early drafts of this book to friends in the hope of soliciting constructive feedback. The response I got was unprecedented. Turns out people have a lot to say about women in the church. Some of my beta readers sent me pages of detailed notes, and for this I am truly grateful. How fitting that a book extolling the blessings of partnership should benefit from such excellent collaboration.

I would like to thank the following people who provided feedback: Nizam Khan, Kristi Gorrod, Helen Kearney, Paul Woodrich, Erik and Robbie Grangaard, Moses Kawuma, Michael Scroggs and Nancy Ford, Rick and Judi Manis, Marlene Ann and J. Bradley Reed, Julia and Nolan Vockrodt, Sandra McCollom, Kevin and Cathy Barnett, Jenifer Powell, and Aney Mathew.

The stunning cover by Safeer Ahmed survived a tough design competition that attracted more than a hundred entries; Nancy Haight did a superb job with the proofreading; and Steve Hackman did a far better job recording the audiobook than I could have done.

As always, I am grateful to my amazing wife Camilla for her unfailing support and guidance. Every book I write, and this one in particular, is a testament to her grace and wisdom.

I write full-time about the gospel of grace, and most of what I write is given away for free. Thanks to the generosity of patrons on Patreon and Donorbox, the good news that I preach is heard in every country on earth. Patrons are partners in this gospel, and without their support, books like this would not be possible. For sharing the journey, heartfelt thanks to Aaron Ashby, Abhishek Chougule, Adam Goldfinch, Adam Tanti, Adriaan Hattingh, Al Babcock , Al Jennings, Alejandro Cantu, Alex Thomas, Alison Gilbert, Alonzo Garcia, Amanda Henderson, Andre de Haan, Andrew Maulding, Andy Manuel, Aney Mathew, Angela Golingi , Anna Thevaos, Annalee Reyes, Anne H. Hoover, Anne Lyttle, Anthony Collins, Arie Duister, Ashley Guzman, Asit Parida, Bank Akinmola, Ben Dailey,

Benny Sunjaya, Beverly Bowman, Bik Hou, Bill Fowler, Bill Pruitt, Bill Shoemaker, Bob Baker, Bob Fricke, Bob Paroski, Bobby Jean Perry, Bonnie Weaver, Brandon Petrowski, Brandon Scott, Brian Jones, Brian Page, Brocton Rye, Bruce Fulton, Bruce Leane, Bruno Dammann, Burandt Adam, Caleb Brubaker, Carl & Sara Petee, Carol Cronin, Carolyn Coates, Cary Geno, Cathy Barnett, Cecil H. Paxton, Cecilia Lim, Cesar & Anna, Chad M. Mansbridge, Charles & Sheilla van Wijk, Cherine Rossman, Chris Esparza, Christopher Gordon, Christopher Johnson, Claude (Bill) Schanuel, Cliff, Clint Byars, Collins K. Raj, Connie-Louise Alexander, Corinna von der Mahlen, Cory Smith, Craig Hunt, Crisostomo L. Martin, Cristopher Suyam, Dale Edwards, Dana Daigle, Daniel Clarke, Danielle Cronje, Danilo Schehrer, Dave Orrison, Dave Parrish, Dave Tremblay, David Aaleskjaer, David Abique, David Cheong, David Edwardds, David Nelson, David S., David Slayback, David Sztrimbely, David Wong, David York, Dawn Strom, Debby Katz, Deborah Long, Debra Hardy, Deirdre M. Rogers, Denise, Denise Kaitala, Dennis & Denise Capra, Derrick Darden, Diane & Eli Listort, Diane Kitson, Diane Peterson, Diane Roman, Diane Schakola, Dollice Chua, Don Beeson, Donna Sweigart, Dottie Hicks, Ed Anderson, Ed Crenshaw, Ed Elliott, Ed N. Diane Pacheco, Eddie C. Livingston P.E., Edward McCarthy, Elaine DeLones, Elly Kraai, Emanuel Bulugu, Eric & Nancy Holman, Eric Thon, Erik Grangaard, Erika & Klaus Degen, Esther van Dijk, Fayrene Sherritt, Frederick Johannes Botha, Garry D. Pifer, Gary Wells, Geoff Powell, Georg Zonnchen, Geraldine Unger, Gerry Macabuhay, Gilbert Gatdula, Gilly Stott, Ginger Banks, Giselle Russell-Clarke, Glenda B. Crawford, Gord Penner, Grace Grace, Graham Irwin, Greg Morneau, Greg & Raelene Race, Gregory K. Hinkle, Hannah Hoffmann, Hayley Jordan, Heather Gill, Helen Kearney, Helen Leafa, Henry HS. Yeo, Ian Wright, Ilva Sturlese, Jack & Janet Surrett, James Davis, James Goss, James Kerr, James Miller, James Mullier, James Thompson, James W. Smith, James Yaranon, Jan Botten, Jana Mings, Jane Hunckler, Janice Best Bright, Jarod & Anita Darashah-Borman, Jason Eugene, Jason foo, Jax Hill, J. Bradley & Marlene Reed, J.B. Lardizabal, Jeffrey, Jenifer Powell, Jennifer Herkommer, Jer Wei Low, Jerry Weinhausen, Jerry Williams, Jim

Firzlaff, Jim Gaines, Jim Powell, Joe May, John Adriaans, John Gardner, John Williams, Jon & Shannon Bonner, Jon Onabowu, Jonathan Gould, JoNell, Jordan Hammond, Joseph Adedeji, Josh Ball, Joyce Rapier, Juan Batule Cabana, Judy C. Ervien, Judy Krug, Julia Vockrodt, Justin Hopper, Karen Moffett, Kath Wells, Kathleen Ault, Kathy Haecker, Katie Bearden, Keith Forwith, Keith Pinke, Ken Spicer, Kenneth Crum, Kenneth Saul, Kent Gilge, Kevin McAllister, Kim Gehring, Kimberly Grigsby, Kimberly Russell, Kitty Kata, KL. Oei, Ko Fi, KP. Wong, Kristi Gorrod, Larissa Hamel, Larry & Helen Wilgus, Laurence Brill, Leon C. Bramlett III, Leonard John Ransil, Lew Gervais, Lewis Sage, Lidia, Linda Essaff, Linda Gerrard, Lisa Reveley, Liz Collard, Lloyd D. McCaskill, Lois Granbery, Lukas Vorberg, Lyle Geck, Lyn Packer, Lynn Alford, Lynne Logan-Pye, M. Caleb Sannoh, Marg & Merv Knott, Margaret Eargle, Margaret Miller, Maria Sanders, Marie, Marie Robison, Marion Carter, Mark & Mary Beth Cain, Mark Wolfe, Marnie, Marshall Kim, Mary Ellen Serafine, Mary Salisbury, Mathavan Rajkumar, Mel and Clare Sanders, Melanie Theilig, Melissa Okonski, Melissa Shands, Mia Young, Michael Folsom, Michael Gragg, Michael & Julie Lipparelli, Michael Kelehan, Michael & Kim Vizza, Michael Miller, Michael Morimando, Michael Scroggs, Michelle, Michelle Cormier, Michelle Lavette French, Mikael Jonsson, Millie Morrison, Moses S. M. Kawuma, Nancy Paquette Poulin, Nata Isr, Neal Hall, Nelson, Nick Atkins, Nizam Khan, Norah Brown, Norin Lumungking-Weier & Justin Weier, Oladipo Awoyinfa, Ore Ijinigba, Oscar Rios, Pagasa De Mesa, Patricia Walker, Patty VanderVeen, Paul & Chantale Roxanas, Paul Burton, Paul F. Eilers, Paul Goodwin, Paul Phang, Paul S. Frey, Paul Woodrich, Penny Creery, Peta Donegan, Peter, Peter Brosnan, Peter Dybing, Peter M. Claffey, Philip Yutzy, Prince, Rachelle Reeve, Rachmat Permana, Ralph Kassen, Randall George, Randall Harmon, Randy & Julee Armstrong, Randy & Shandra Montague, Raymond Glossop, Real Paquette, Rebekah K. Watson, Red Burgos, Rene Bouwer, Renee Woodward, Rhea Cooper, Richard F. De Souza, Richard Lee, Richard W. Evans, Rick Cowdery, Rick & Judi Manis, Ricky L. Cain, Rita Collins, Rob Blanshard, Robert Jones, Robert Marshall, Robin Waller, Roland Stamey, Ron Clark, Ron Roudebush,

Ronan, Roshan Easo, Ruth Coulthard, S. H. Lee, S. Kunnath, Sam Bouwer, Samia Causley, Samuel Lowell, Sara Wilson Hughes, Sarah, Sharon Collins, Sharon Stark, Shelly Hakspiel, Si Na, Simon Brown, Solly San Juan, Stella Emmanuel, Stephanie Kirtland, Stephanie Turney, Stephen Caldwell, Steve Espamer, Steve & Sandra McCollom, Steven J. Shane, Steven Mann, Sue Crissman, Sue Gardner, Susan Coleman, Susan Scalisi, Susie Dunlap, Tamara Barker, Tanya Nareau, Ted Nelson, Terry Maupin, Terry and Janelle Myers, Terry Tripp, Tertia Oosthuizen, Theodore Heintzelman, Theresa M. Benischek, Thierry Bras, Tina McIntire, Tom & Kay Stocking, Tom Ludemann, Tom Tepandi, Tommy, Tony Cutty, Tony Ide, Tony Vogel, Toshiko Johnson, Travis Taylor, Trevor Lovegrove, Trice Seargent, Wesley Matsell, Will McCulloch, William Conroy, William Lowery, and Yvonne Beukes.

Award-winning books by Paul Ellis

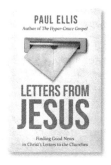

Winner (Christian Indie Awards)
Finalist (International Book Awards)

The letters from Jesus to the Revelation churches must be the most misunderstood chapters in the Bible. Many dismiss them as too hard, too strange, or too scary. In *Letters from Jesus*, Paul Ellis unpacks the unqualified good news found in these letters from heaven!

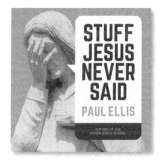

Gold Medal (Illumination Book Awards)
Book of the Year (Christian Small Publishers)

If the stuff Jesus never said is the stuff you thought he said, then the stuff he did say may surprise you! Using paintings from the great masters, *Stuff Jesus Never Said* shatters the myth of the angry, fault-finding God and celebrates the God that Christ revealed—a God who wants you to prosper and live well.

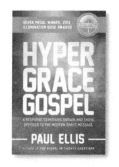

Silver Medal (Illumination Book Awards)

Just as you cannot measure the universe, you cannot fathom the limits of God's love for you. God's grace for you exceeds your wildest dreams. Drawing on insights gleaned from more than forty grace preachers, *The Hyper-Grace Gospel* addresses common misperceptions some have about the message of grace. This book will leave you marveling at the relentless love of your Father.

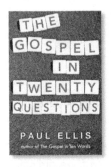